Revival, Racism, & Rapture
A Fireside Reflection on Culture and Times

"Joe has done it again. As an apostolic leader for the Kentucky Assemblies of God ministers and churches, Dr. Girdler has drawn from his life and ministry experiences to provide the church with a great resource on how to lead and respond to cultural issues with biblical clarity. This work is a beneficial resource for those who want to lead well."

—**Rev. Doug Clay**
General Superintendent, Assemblies of God – USA
Springfield, MO

"Dr. Girdler's book is a thought-provoking read meant to stimulate conversation regarding various topics addressed. The topics provide a theological thread woven throughout the book, ultimately challenging the reader to fall on his or her face and seek after God. Dr. Girdler is an emerging voice concerning the workings of the Holy Spirit, coupled with his desire to see the body of Christ realize its full potential. Not only will this book enrich the life of the Church, I know it will also become a staple in Bible College classrooms."

—**Rev. Dr. Adam C. Sikorski**
Associate Professor, North Central University
Minneapolis, MN

"My friend, Joe Girdler, has written yet another book that captured my attention immediately in the Introduction—I couldn't put it down! It is a moving, engaging and delightful read. He covers a variety of subjects like leadership, racism, COVID-19, and revival! His writing style masterfully weaves all this together for a winning read. Chapter 5 on "Leadership Principles" is excellent, especially for emergent leaders."

—**Rev. Gary Grogan**
U40 Director, Illinois District Assemblies of God
Urbana, IL

"This book is more than a quick read for information. It is a prophetic call for our hearts to be set on fire for another spiritual awakening. The passion of the author is contagious. When writing on racism, Dr. Girdler refuses to relegate his concerns to platitudes when he says, 'We don't have to say things perfectly; I simply need to have the conversation.' This apostolic voice from Kentucky is a timely word for 2020 and beyond."

—**Rev. Dr. Bob Rhoden**
Forty Years of Pastoral and Denominational Leadership
Glen Allen, VA

"Having served under Pastor Joe's leadership in the Kentucky Ministry Network, I can with confidence assert that his passion and drive for the manifest presence of God shines through his writing. Common theological themes run through this book. He traces the impact of revival experiences upon his life personally, examines markers of historical revivals, and shows the current need for a revival in our COVID-19 journey. *Thank you, Pastor Joe, for the personal challenge of awakening me spiritually.* As you read these pages, be prepared for a challenge and response for such a time as this."

—**Dr. Garry Brackett**
Executive Director, Shepherds Advantage, Inc.
Indianapolis, IN

"For most pastors and church leaders, genuine revival and cultural relevancy are two areas of ministry often allusive and unattainable. This book offers history and context that inspires hope and provides the practical to partner with God's presence and activity in the local church. Dr. Girdler details past revivals for readers with a front row seat to history and the opportunity to consider what God desires to do socially and spiritually in this current generation. I finished the book filled with expectancy and confidence that others will do the same."

—**Rev. Terry Crigger**
Assistant Superintendent, Kentucky Assemblies of God
Senior Pastor, Christ's Chapel Assembly of God
Erlanger, KY

"Pastor Joe Girdler offers us a powerful reflection regarding the nature of revival. Written from the perspective of long personal experience, Joe leads us on a bracing but refreshing pilgrimage that combines the testimony of the past and the challenges of the present. His details about revival history, his candor with respect to his own ministry journey, and his Kentucky horse sense for sound leadership will surely bless the heart that is hungry and thirsty for righteousness."

—**Dr. David Thomas, Ph.D.**
Missionary and Professor of Bible
Assemblies of God World Missions

"This book challenges its readers to embrace a biblical posture when faced with current societal issues. Pastor Girdler's prophetic voice beckons the reader to a deep commitment and to live out their faith in tangible ways, understanding that although "we are drowning in information, but we are starving for wisdom." May the Lord grant us His wisdom! This book is a much-needed resource for today's church. Thank you, Pastor Joe!"

—**Rev. Elly C. Marroquin**
National Director of Christian Education and Discipleship
General Council of the Assemblies of God
Springfield, MO
Endorsement credit style

Revival, Racism, & Rapture
A Fireside Reflection on Culture and Times

Foreword by
Carolyn Tennant, Ph.D.

Joseph S. Girdler

Revival, Racism, & Rapture
A Fireside Reflection on Culture and Times

Copyright © 2021 Joseph S. Girdler

All rights reserved. No portion of this book may be reproduced, stored in a retrieval system, or transmitted in any form or by any means, electronic or mechanical, including photocopying, recording, or by an information storage and retrieval system—except by a reviewer who may quote brief passages in a review to be printed in a magazine or newspaper—without permission in writing from the publisher.

Published in Crestwood, Kentucky by **Meadow Stream Publishing.**

Cover design and Interior Layout by Uberwriters Christian Ghostwriters
www.uberwriters.com

Scripture quotations marked (NLT) are taken from the Holy Bible, New Living Translation, copyright © 1996, 2004, 2015 by Tyndale House Foundation. Used by permission of Tyndale House Publishers, Inc., Carol Stream, Illinois 60188. All rights reserved.

Scripture quotations marked (ESV) are from the ESV® Bible (The Holy Bible, English Standard Version®), copyright © 2001 by Crossway Bibles, a publishing ministry of Good News Publishers. Used by permission. All rights reserved.

Scripture quotations marked (KJV) are from The Authorized (King James) Version. Rights in the Authorized Version in the United Kingdom are vested in the Crown. Reproduced by permission of the Crown's patentee, Cambridge University Press.

Scripture quotations marked (TLB) are taken from The Living Bible copyright © 1971. Used by permission of Tyndale House Publishers, a Division of Tyndale House Ministries, Carol Stream, Illinois 60188. All rights reserved.

Scripture quotations marked (NIV) are taken from the Holy Bible, New International Version®, NIV®. Copyright © 1973, 1978, 1984, 2011 by Biblica, Inc.™ Used by permission of Zondervan. All rights reserved worldwide. www.zondervan.com The "NIV" and "New International Version" are trademarks registered in the United States Patent and Trademark Office by Biblica, Inc.™

ISBN 978-1-7379913-4-2 Paperback

ISBN 978-1-7379913-5-9 eBook

Dedication

This book is dedicated to my wife, Renee'. She means everything to me.

There is no beauty brighter than a virtuous heart. Renee's heart is the purest I've known. She sits at 5:00 a.m. most mornings, Bible in hand, coffee within reach, praying over a handwritten list of needs and names, desperate for answers and God's touch. I am convinced that many have found strength for their tomorrow because she's prayed for them today. Many times in our marriage I have often sensed that she ministers to more people in her medical clinic than I do in my church (previously) or other ministry assignment(s). Her faith is unshakable. Her colleagues and patients know it. Our family finds strength in it.

From Renee', I learned to trust in God but to still lock the front and back doors to our home. It is true that not everybody has pure motives.

This year we're married thirty-five years. Months ago, I came through the most challenging hospitalization, complications, and health concerns thus faced in my journey. I couldn't have made it through without her consistent love and care. She brought a new meaning to me in the concept of "home health". After two months of declining and weakening health, honestly wondering at times myself if I were going to live for the long haul, she came into our bedroom in the early morning hours of a Sunday morning and prayed over me while I still rested. When I awakened later in the morning, she told me "today was going to be the day of breakthrough." After not eating more than 3-5 sips of broth a day for eight long weeks, midday I sensed for the first time that I could eat something. It was only ten bites that day, granted, but I ate. And, daily the Lord strengthened me from then forward.

Commitment to the Lord and to the inescapable fact that He put us together from the moment I saw her is the secret to our love's longevity. I am wholly devoted to this woman. She stops me in my tracks. When we met those many years ago, I had been searching for something deeper in my relationship with God. I was continually meeting "Spirit-filled" Christians whose depth of faith mesmerized me and surpassed anything I had known previously of the spiritual matters of life. What exactly was meant by the term, "Spirit-filled?" Weren't all Christians Spirit-filled? I sat alone in the back of a church, having been invited by a friend. For the first time in my life, I tangibly detected the presence of God.

Weeks later in that same church, I looked rows ahead. There was the most beautiful girl I had ever seen, but what struck me even more was her tender heart for the Lord. To this day, Renee's walk with God overshadows any prayer or faith I've ever attained.

She is my inspiration and is my strength for weathering any storm. She is the most thorough in any calculating situation. At times she can be anxiously intense. It's all balanced with her gift of rich intercessory prayer. In my darkest hours she shines light. Traveling globally for years, I can sense her heartbeat from a thousand miles away. When away on countless travels my heart stays with my love. I have responded hundreds of times to those who would ask, "How are you, Pastor?" with the words, "If Renee' still loves me, and my kids are okay, I'm okay."

Thank you, Renee', for being everything to me.

All my love, Joe

Table of Contents

Acknowledgments xi

Foreword xv

Introduction xvii

Chapter 1 Do They See Jesus in Me? 1

Chapter 2 Revival at Cane Ridge, Paris, KY (1801) 7

Chapter 3 Revival at Asbury College, Wilmore, KY (1970) 27

Chapter 4 Revival at King's Way Assembly, Versailles, KY (1997) 47

Chapter 5 Leading For Revival 71

Chapter 6 Suffering, Serving, and Seeking Throughout a Pandemic 81

Chapter 7 Rapture? Mark of the Beast? 93

Chapter 8 An Appointed Time 105

Chapter 9 Race Relations (2020) 117

Chapter 10 The Prayer 129

Resources 135

About the Author 147

Endnotes 161

Acknowledgments

With special thanks:

* TO my pastor. I count it a privilege to have interviewed for this book my pastor during my university years when I met Jesus in a most radical way, Rev. Ken Groen. While researching the historical revival at Asbury College. Asbury Revival attendee, Pastor Groen, now retired as a former Regional Superintendent for the Open Bible Churches of America and living in Des Moines, Iowa, with his wife, Nadine, offered a personal account of the revival from his own experiences and recollections.

His church's (First Assembly of God, Lexington, Kentucky) rapid growth was a testimony during my undergraduate years to how Pastor Ken and Nadine Groen worked seamlessly together as a team—loving and discipling people and challenging them for global impact. Theirs was the first church where I had actually seen international and local missions emphasis blended, as it were, aligning with the heartbeat of God. Revival was not merely a series of services under this shepherd's leadership but changed lives—people of multiple demographics, races, and ethnicities sitting side by side in every row of that church.

* TO Asbury University Library Director, Dr. Morgan Tracy; Archive Librarian, Suzanne Gehring; and Library Circulation Supervisor, Patty MacFarland.

* TO Dr. Carolyn Tennant for her magnetic love of revivals. I've been a student of revival for years, but during my doctoral studies she became a mentor and trusted colleague who brought endless encouragement to my writing. This book places the Asbury Revival experience in the context of *nine characteristics of revival* by renowned revival student and lecturer, Dr. Carolyn Tennant. Dr. Tennant's efforts in the field of revival as a scholar at North Central University and The Assemblies of God Theological Seminary, her first hand accounts of the Argentine Revival, as well as her serving as a trusted voice and member

of her denomination's Council on the Commission on Doctrines and Practices, lends immeasurable credence to the project.

* TO my professors and seminarians of Asbury Theological Seminary in the 1980s that challenged my young mind for deeper things of God.

* TO missionaries Paul Brannan, Rocky Grams, Martin Jacobson, the late Steve Hill, and Ralph Hiatt for added history given through their personal encouragement or written words and for their years of dedicated global missions service that set the foundation for my own Argentine experiences.

* TO my gifted editor always at the top of her game, Dr. Lois Olena.

* TO the astute insights of Uberwriters professionals, Brad and Hilton Rahme with their offices in Louisville, KY and Cape Town, South Africa. They made more than an impact. They made a difference for this work you read today.

* TO the members, faithful worshipers, and genuine seekers of an exceptional congregation I was privileged to pastor in the 1990s and early 2000s: King's Way Assembly, Versailles/Lexington, Kentucky. Our family's years there fostered my heart for authentic revival, purity, holy reverence, Spirit-filled worship experiences, integrity in ministry, and a sense that the manifest presence of God changes everything.

* TO the many across the nations who lifted prayers for me during a most challenging three-month season of health complications and recuperation from postoperative surgery and subsequent Covid-19 diagnosis.

* TO revival seekers across the globe who tirelessly pursue God's presence. I've been with many of you in your churches and nations. You inspire me. Your vision and hunger for making disciples strengthens all those around you. Your relentless and passionate prayers and worship of the One True God further holds up arms that are weary and gives refuge from any battle.

* TO – most of all - Father God, for Your unfailing love;

Acknowledgments

* TO Jesus, my King and Savior, who gave His life that I and mine might live; To You, Holy Spirit, for Your marvelous power, comfort, instruction, and intimate companionship never leaving or abandoning me. All my life You have been faithful to me.

Foreword

Dr. Joseph S. Girdler is the superintendent of the Kentucky Ministry Network of the Assemblies of God, and that apostolic calling assuredly has its full weight of responsibilities, lessons, and demands. In spite of the import of that position, however, those of us who know him well recognize him to be a true gentleman in the sense of being a "gentle man." One can't say that about a lot of people these days when rancor abounds, offense surfaces easily, and people can obliterate one another in a heartbeat.

Rather Pastor Joe, as he humbly calls himself, is a wise man who oozes the fruit of the Spirit and truly cares for people. He is a real "leader-servant" in a world where that title is easily thrown around, while its meaning often stops merely at being willing to set up chairs for an event.

With Pastor Joe, you know you are being thought about and prayed for. You get a note or a text with an encouraging word out of the blue. The message indicates he has put himself in your shoes, and he nails where you are at. He is aware of people and their needs and manages to minister to your heart. I have wondered how such an active leader can find the time to do this, but he prioritizes people over a lifestyle of frantic busyness. He takes time to think, pray, worship, and hear from God.

With the rarity of people like this being what it is, the thought comes to my mind from time to time that it would be ever so nice just to sit down with Pastor Joe and have a chat. I can picture myself in his home with a misty Kentucky morning backdrop, sitting in an easy chair by the fire. That is the exact tone of this warm little tome you are about to read. It is an opportunity to pick this gentleman's brain about his beautiful home state and what God has done here. Talk would never stray far from spiritual matters because that is how Pastor Joe thinks and lives. He would be applying Truth to contemporary situations: to COVID-19, to race relations, to the end times, and to thoughts of an upcoming revival as well as what God has done in the past in what is almost his backyard.

As with any conversation, we would swerve around a little. One thread would take us off into another related idea and then another and thus we would come back to the first thread again and somehow it would all weave together. We would come away full.

Pastor Joe's heart to see the Spirit of God move today in our land is strong. He is a transparent man who is willing to share both victories and weaknesses as well as God's work in all of it. We won't stray far from Kentucky horse farm country, even getting in the car and taking some side trips.

Come on along. There's an easy chair waiting by the fire saved just for you, and the presence of God will be invited as well.

By **Dr. Carolyn Tennant**

Professor Emerita, North Central University, Minneapolis; and adjunct professor in the D.Min. program at the Assemblies of God Theological Seminary, Springfield, MO.

Introduction

What if you walked into your church for your service and suddenly discovered an atmosphere where the Holy Spirit was acceptably permitted to do whatsoever He wants? What if worship leaders were concerned less with their worship set lists and more with finding God's manifest presence? What if you heard the underlying roar of prayer and praise rather than receiving the simple greeting of a handshake from someone at the door? The typical and superficial "hello" to a casual friend followed by sitting down and waiting is replaced with you being drawn to the worship team's Spirit-led melodies. You see people intimately meeting with the Lord at the altar, some weeping silently, others calling out for their families and for revival. Others are pacing throughout the aisles –walking as they pray. What if guests, rather than thinking that this seems odd, strange, or weird, thought to themselves, "Wow, this is an overwhelming presence of God?" What if pastors walked circumspectly to the pulpit cautiously waiting –with that ever so tilted ear- to hear the nudging of the Lord for His service? What if we waited just a moment standing in the pulpit and lingered in God's presence before rushing on to our pre-set service agenda? What if worship leaders and worship teams sang more songs to the Lord than about the Lord?

    The overarching theme of this book is that of a renewed great awakening and genuine revival. The Psalmist had deep hunger for renewal and revival as he passionately gave us in Psalm 119: 145-152). I have welcomed you to a fireside chat with varying conversation topics that thread throughout these chapters. Understanding revival through historical accounts aids us in grasping revival reality amidst our rapidly changing culture. Many people in today's society are drowning in information but starving for wisdom. On a lighter side, yet totally related, I laughed some years ago when a minister said to me, "The more I get to know people, the more I realize why Noah only let animals on the boat."

Living in a family of physicians I've learned that doctors don't make you healthy. My dad was a teacher but I learned that teachers don't make you learn. I've lived through the decades of the health and fitness craze. Still, I became obese. I've heard it said that trainers don't make you fit. And, with professional athletes making into the multi-millions – far more than their piece of the pie – it remains true. Coaches don't make you rich. At some point each of us has to realize our own responsibility for where we are – where we want to be – and where we want to go. Many are diamonds in the rough awaiting their God-called destiny. Conditions do not determine one's destiny. Their decisions do. I've had hundreds of conversations through the years with people about what they want to do in life. The most important thing in life is not what one becomes. It's who they become.

> *Many people in today's society are drowning in information but starving for wisdom.*

You are God's chosen with a purposed destiny. What a gift to have life – today. How will you make a difference? Start your day by offering everything in it to God. Ask Him to empty you so you can find more of Him. When you have grown past what God can give you and worship Him for Who He is, He will be most adored through your life. Be grateful for the small things, the big things, the hard things, and the everyday things. There's always someone struggling more than you or I. Find peace and contentment in your situation. It's calming, stilling, even serene knowing that sometimes my plans are not meant to work out. His plans are all that matter. When I let worry, anxiety, apprehension, burdens, concerns, and uneasiness control my emotions it is as if I don't have enough faith in God to take care of it. Remember, God is preparing you for something great. Hold on. Be patient. God hears your prayers. He has it all worked out. He seals you in His protection.

> "The animals going in were male and female of every living thing, as God had commanded Noah. Then the LORD shut him in" (Genesis 7:16, NIV).

Introduction

The animals entered the ark, both male and female, of every living thing as God commanded. But then it was God Himself who sealed the door, shut Noah and his family inside. Noah didn't have the options of which lock or latch he preferred on the door apparently. God shut him in. He sealed them inside. I want to be sealed inside His protection. I want the Lord to seal me within His ark of provision, protection, and purpose. You don't keep yourself safe. In His will He seals you for His purpose. He is the God of endless worth. God is patient. He is kind. His ways are superior. His is God Almighty. His kingdom stands alone.

My hope is to offer something of substance that brings you, today's leaders, pointed insight for the things you will face in your work for the Lord. Leaders should expect the spiritual gift of discernment to work as readily as the other gifts of the Spirit. The Church must embrace altogether the talents and gifts designed and given by God. Casting vision for a holy standard brings tangible transformation. When leaders and churches walk in the Spirit everything changes. If there was ever a time the Church needed to hear and find the voice of God it is today. His freedom awaits you.

Surveying experiences of indicated revival, an examination of historical pattern, aids us in ascertaining our role in any emerging move of God. Some may ask, "Is revival possible for this generation?" The erosion of moral fortitude and mounting spiritual regression is not a new phenomenon. What we experience today is readily recognizable from generations past. Is it possible there are generational cycles that lead God to call-out evangelists, pastors, teachers, prophets and apostles to deliver nations from spiritual destruction?

Faithful followers of Christ across the nations diligently pray for a spiritual awakening once again. I recently attended a gathering of ministers praying for our nation. I listened attentively as one after another of the men and women prayed against growing immorality, lawlessness, wickedness, corruption, and deception. Others prayed that racism would miraculously come to an end. Another prayed that America would see the laws legalizing abortion overturned. And, another prayed that elitism would be eradicated and equality would be available for all.

Some wonder if the church has been silent far too long in believing again for holiness among God's people, repentance in the church, and forgiveness of one for another. Too many leaders live fulfilled and comfortable as commonplace or routine Christian managers rather than as the apostolic leaders God intended for their lives and His Church. Today's churchgoers appear shallow on holiness. Pulpits are filled with those who hold the gifts rather than those who hold the keys.

For those believing revival is not only possible, but reality from generation to generation, prayers are faithfully heard for prodigals and the backslidden, for the next generation church, for the brightest of our young people to receive a call to ministry, and for a harvest of souls for Christ. Those blinded in their sin are but a testimony away from finding freedom in Christ. Love them for who they are and share your life-giving hope in Christ. Though the emphasis for holiness and righteousness seems to have taken a backseat in mainstream Christendom as I've traveled Kentucky and the nation(s), I am encouraged to sense next-gen leaders are an army arising. There are 21st century churches that humbly strive for integrity and character before the Lord. I've been there. I've seen them. I've prayed with them. I've worshipped with them. I've preached among them. And, thousands of them are millennial, gen-X'rs, and gen-Z'rs.

As faith and doctrine builders, perhaps one of the clearest functions of an apostolic leader is that they serve as spiritual parents in fostering and developing the next generation of priestly leaders. Recognizing the need for an anointed generation of Pentecostal leaders and in no way lessening the calling of God for the preaching ministry, a changing society has opened numerous platforms to share Christ in ways never before conceived. With an ever-shifting culture, the Church struggles to embrace out-of-the-box thinkers and those who pursue new ministry endeavors not yet known to accepted structures. The twenty-first-century Church's most endearing legacy well may be that we began to

Introduction

reflect on opportunities and act in accordance of reaching the lost by accepting and experiencing ministry through venues of new wineskins.

Revival is an authentic move of the Spirit that changes individual's lives, church communities, and large segments of society itself. Whether one studies the past revivals from Azusa, to Argentina, to the Hebrides, the Asbury revival, or those of Amy Semple McPherson, Oral Roberts, Kathryn Kuhlman, Billy Graham, or Maria Woodsworth-Etter, Whitefield, or Wesley, you'll find deep prayer, rich repentance, and wide-sweeping community impact. Systematic community change, apostolic advancement, and individualistic and corporate creativity are innovations by the regenerating work of the Holy Spirit. Just as there is an individual anointing and – I also believe – a corporate anointing, there is personal revival that moves men and women to make a difference in the lives of those they encounter. There is likewise corporate revival that distinguishes itself and mobilizes groups to renewal and revitalization. There are also those things confronted that thwart all of the above. The pages to follow will allow you an inside look to three distinct revival encounters and more. I have attended multiple revival services in my years of church-attendance and ministry. I have seen churches decades previously and within months most recently living revival. It can be. And, you can experience God's manifest presence in your life and ministries as well. In the chapters ahead we'll explore various pieces of this often-puzzling revival topic through a myriad of intertwined themes.

As in each of my previously published books, various personal and intimate storylines are woven throughout the manuscript allowing the reader a front-row glimpse into fragments of my own narrative.

This is my story…

It was the summer of 1989 when Renee' and I first visited Argentina. The series of tent meetings being conducted just west of Buenos Aires (BA) was designed around a medical team from the United States offering complimentary health care for locals.

It was in a barrio named Moro'n, approximately twenty-two miles from the center of the Buenos Aires metropolis. Renee' was a member of the medical team. The hope was for a church to be planted with the people of the area after we served and ministered during the week. Missionaries Ron and Terri Pitts and Argentine pastor, Moises Barrientos, led the efforts. Not being medical myself, I spent my week playing soccer and developing rapports with neighborhood kids on dirt fields near the tent. Relationship evangelism remains a personal passion today.

It was in Argentina that I saw revival as I had never known it before.

It was in Argentina that I saw revival as I had never known it before. While this book is not about Argentina, it was there that I initially encountered impacting moments and memories that followed me to the pastorate I would lead just three years later.

Subsequent to our tent campaign, the church that was planted continued to grow, land was purchased, and a large ministry development became a reality for Centro Familiar El Kyrios. And, ... Pastor Moises? At this writing, he's now the treasurer of the Argentine Assemblies of God National Missions Department.

Immediately upon returning to our small, rented apartment in Lexington, Kentucky, I knew I had to find a way back to this enchanting land. Twelve months later, I returned for a second visit to Argentina and discerned yet again—quite simply—that something supernatural was taking place. This specific tent campaign, in Temperley, about eighteen miles from BA, was in the district of Lomas de Zamora and was coordinated with Argentine pastor, Edgardo Munoz, and missionaires, Dick and Cynthia Nicholson. Today, Pastor Edgardo is the Argentine Assemblies of God Christian Education Director and Vice Director of the famed Rio de la Plata Bible Institute, led by long-term missionary educators, Rocky and Sherry Grams. Rocky had previously spent sixteen years in Bolivia planting churches with his parents high in the Andes. Today, the BA Bible school has

Introduction

graduated over four thousand trained pastors and evangelists over seventy-five years, changing the spiritual landscape across the globe for the Lord's work. The church from this Temperley outreach today has an estimated attendance of well over 1,200 and both of the tent campaigns mentioned have become two of the strongest missions churches in the Argentine Assemblies of God.

What I experienced from both journeys was soon to be known as The Argentine Revival where countless souls were changed by God's manifest presence. Missionary evangelists, Steve and Jeri Hill arrived in Argentina in the mid 1980s, as told to me by the thirty-three-year Argentina missionary veteran, Martin Jacobson. With a number of national pastors, Hill had founded the Patagonia Bible Institute, where Jacobson later served as Director. Argentine evangelist, Carlos Annacondia, seemed to be leading what could be understood as the first wave of this revival outpouring. Steve later became a household name across the nations to those who sought revival and renewal. His transformative and mesmerizing messages drew thousands from around the globe to the Brownsville, Florida, Father's Day 1995 revival that lasted six years.

Not until 2014 did I have the opportunity to return in ministry to Argentina. Martin and Charlotte Jacobson had left BA years earlier for the deep southern cone, Patagonia, to develop the Patagonia Bible Institute. Ministering primarily at this Bible college for their Spiritual Emphasis Week, I again experienced among the students and in churches where I ministered the same hunger and passion for God's outpouring as I had witnessed twenty-five years earlier.

One evening, at a sizeable church where I had been invited to preach, over 500 people came to an altar when I provided an opportunity to respond to the message. The translator leaned to me and whispered, "Pastor, you do recognize, right, that every single one of these people expects you to individually pray with them before you leave?" It was already getting late into the evening. I smiled and quickly settled into what I had not anticipated. For the next hours we ministered to each person, one at a time. I will certainly not neglect nor forget the puddles of tears on the concrete flooring of that church's altar area, as those hungry souls adored and worshipped the Lord in repentance and reverence.

Whether you read about Argentine revivalists, Carlos Annacondia, Claudio Freidzon, or names who preached good news in Argentina a century earlier like Allen Gardiner, R. Edward Miller, and more, you will find common threads: powerful commitment to the Holy Spirit and His work, powerful preaching of God's Word, commanding testimonies of individuals touched by God, and prevailing prayer. It sounds the makings of revival to me.

Alicia Wood was the first Assemblies of God missionary to serve in Argentina. She studied from early Azusa Street leaders and received the baptism of the Holy Spirit in 1909, propelling her remarkable ministry journey ahead. Nearly fifty years later, a sixty-two-day revival campaign of 1954, led by evangelist Tommy Hicks, set a further foundation and framework for what was yet to come.

In the 1970s, missionaries Paul and Betty Brannan and the late, Ralph and Frances Hiatt (the Hiatts first came to Argentina in 1965 and served nearly forty years) were used significantly as church planters and tent campaign revivalists. Their call to deep commitment to the Lord filled altars with tears and hearts yearning to impact the nations. Later in this book you will read of a three-month season in the mid-1990s (approximately ninety days) when revival filled the church I had pastored. I have learned much of what I know and the passion I carry for missions from Paul and Betty Brannan. At the time my church was experiencing revival they had returned from the mission field and were also pastoring – at that time - a Kentucky church thirty minutes from my location. Simultaneously, they experienced a revival outpouring that lasted nearly two years. Similar geographic locations and synchronized timing of revivals is yet another gripping element of the Lord's work through revival, itself.

Introduction

With the Argentina experiences in my background and in my heart and spirit, initial considerations of this book were birthed while pastoring that local congregation in the greater Lexington, Kentucky region just prior to the year 2000 (Y2K). Chapters are a collection of revivalist introspections mingled with three specific and lengthier insights from distinct representative Kentucky revivals, each containing specified bibliographies and sources for further individual study. You'll read detailed facts from the legendary Second Great Awakening's Cane Ridge Revival, the renowned 1970 Asbury College Revival, and more.

This book is not an all-inclusive examination or the sole guide for the complex matters addressed. Certainly, contextualization is critical for both practical and scriptural preaching ministry, as well as the development and implementation of leadership character and philosophy. It will help current and established church leaders better configure their personal ethos on themes offered, for the sole purpose that others may discover the manifest presence of God. Further, Paul admonished us in Philippians chapter 2 to be keenly sensitive to the interests and needs of others. Caring for others is the Christ-like thing to do.

> *I write for the generations to come who will someday read about revival for the first time.*

Additionally, I write for the generations to come who will someday read about revival for the first time to help them better understand such challenges and how leaders should respond regardless of the generations they serve. There is a blueprint inside the DNA of apostolic leaders promising enormous strides for the destiny of God's Church if the mantle is humbly, prayerfully, and scripturally acknowledged, received, and carried out. Both Old and New Testament passages will teach readers of revival the power of the Holy Spirit (see: Genesis 35; 2 Chronicles 15, 23, 24, 34, 35; 2 Kings 11, 12, 22, 23; Ezra 5, 6; Nehemiah 9, 12; Acts 2, 4, 5, 9, 11, 12, 16, 24). As Dr. Jodi Detrick, from the Seattle area and author of *The Jesus-Hearted Woman: 10 Leadership Qualities for Enduring & Endearing Influence*, said when she wrote an endorsement for one of my previous books, "When it comes to ministry life, sometimes what you need is a hand-on-the-shoulder, where-the-rubber-meets-the-road kind of guidance from someone who's been there and lived to tell about it." I trust that this book will be that kind of guidance for everyone who reads this book, but especially for emerging leaders. Dr. Carol Taylor, retired president of Evangel University in Missouri, found this benefit to be true in a former book of mine when she too wrote this comment after reading it: "Insights come from a deep well of lived worship and from nurturing communities in a life of worship—and we are the beneficiaries."

We need revival. God wants to do something magnificent within each of us. Too many settle for the world's standards rather than step into God's ways, which are always higher and always better. Standards are not always rules of legalism. They are banners of Spirit-led living and witness. We have lived far too long beneath our inheritance in Christ. God has more for those who will follow Him than they will ever comprehend. It cannot be imagined what God has in store and has prepared for those who love Him (1 Corinthians 2:9).

> "If my people which are called by my name
> shall humble themselves and pray and seek my face
> and turn from their wicked ways: then will I hear from heaven,
> and will forgive their sin, and will heal their land"
> (2 Chronicles 7:14, KJV).

Chapter 1

Do They See Jesus in Me?

"In the same way, let your light shine before others, so that they may see your good works and give glory to your Father who is in heaven"
(Matthew 5:16, ESV).

Can I have a role in the revival of the modern day church? Religion emphasizes filling churches with people. The Gospel underscores filling people with God.

Early on a sunny February Sunday morning, I stopped the car and entered a local retail chain, one of the few I found open on that already two-hour drive from my Louisville, Kentucky home. Similar to a modern day itinerate horseback-riding preacher of old (as was a distant relative of mine), I was en route to a small rural church to minister God's Word. This brief stop was to purchase a gift for two very special young toddlers— the pastor's sons where I was soon to arrive. After a short walk through the aisles, I exited with six little plastic $1.00 toy dinosaurs; a simple gesture to let the kids know Pastor Joe loved them. Then it struck me, "Will they see Jesus in me?"

> *If true revival came to our generation, would the world recognize it?*

If true revival came to our generation, would the world recognize it? Can people see the fruit of revival-changed lives? There is a message in the way one person treats another. Maybe we should listen more attentively.

Having been a life-long music lover, I listen to music endlessly as I drive long commutes. I often find myself dialed into one of my many go-to Spotify playlists. Before continuing my Sunday morning ministry drive on that February day, I sat for about a half-an-hour in my car at a nearby remote location to simply write the names or words of songs that had spoken to my heart that day on my drive. Words that reminded me in one way or another of the question lingering in my head, "Would these two very special little boys see a difference in me?"

- Do they see Jesus in Me? Do they recognize His face? Do I communicate His love and grace? Do I reflect who He is in the way I choose to be? Do they see Jesus in me? (Joy Williams' song)
- Are you willing to be opened up and broken? Evil throws stones. It's too hard to say you're wrong until you realize you can't go on. Reach beyond the pain. The Lord will search me and look into my heart. (Jaci Velasquez' song, "Flower in the Rain")
- Grace is an awesome commodity. You can see when God opens a door, or when He picks you up. But there are things you cannot see when He shielded you, ... Oh God's grace. You were lost, but now you are found. You would have been hopeless, but His grace set you free. (Clint Brown, "If Not for Grace")
- The Secret: – The power of sin is broken. Jesus has won the victory. Nothing can hold Him down. He is the great and risen King. He's alive. He's arisen. He reigns on high. Sing Hallelujah. He won it all for me and for you. God is for you. Reach to Him and trust Him. (Todd Dulaney, "The Anthem")
- Behold the Lamb, the precious Lamb of God. Holy is the

Lamb. Why He loves us so, we shall never know; He was born into sin that I may live again. (Tamela Mann, "Best Days")

- Teach your people to fall in love with Jesus afresh and anew. Do you love—truly love—to worship the Lord? You must love to worship Him. All night worship gatherings ... or lingering times—to develop intimacy with God. He'll be in that place. There's nobody like Jesus. He inhabits the praises of his people. Oh, His presence. Encourage people to lift their hands—in surrender—to His holiness; then it becomes the lifting of holy hands – not yours—but His; nothing but in honor to His power and grace upon us. (Clint Brown, "I Love to Worship You")
- Rescue the perishing (Fanny Crosby)
- Oh how I love Jesus ...
- Just as I am ...
- This is my story ...
- My Tribute (This song by Nicole C. Mullen was played and sung in my wedding to Renee as she walked down the aisle.)
- When my heart is overwhelmed, lead me to the Rock that is higher than I. (Stephen Hurd, "Lead Me to the Rock")
- He is a strong tower from the enemy; He is a secret place; a sanctuary; He is a hiding place He fills your heart with songs of deliverance when you are afraid ... He is a firm foundation; My salvation; My solid rock; Let the weak say, I am strong in the strength of the Lord; you can trust the Lord. (Selah)
- Nothing remains the same when it's touched by the Lord. All things forever changed when it's touched by God, when we're close to God. Touch me Lord; reach out and touch me, Lord. (Clint Brown)
- No more crying, no more complaining; hands raised in surrender; I will trust the Lord.

- He gives beauty for ashes, strength for fear, gladness for mourning, and peace for despair, when what you've done keeps you from moving, God knows your need. His love and forgiveness are fresh every morning. Your righteousness is solely in Him (yes). What a beautiful promise for the leader to stand on. (Crystal Lewis)

I arrived at the church and enjoyed a day of ministry and preaching the Word of God to this small, rural, diverse, and attentive congregation. I was struck by the three-year-old pastor's son and his concentrated attention to the music, praise, and worship in the service. I thought of six small toy dinosaurs, what I anticipated would be smiles on two little faces, and their likely eagerness to make noises like prehistoric animals, laugh, and play.

I was delighted to have been invited to their home, a parsonage situated just to the side of the church building, to enjoy a meal following the service. There, I presented the simple toys. These two children were some of the best-behaved toddlers I'd yet to meet or encounter, bright beyond imagination, and growing up in a home so filled with love. I thought to myself, "These little one's are destined for great things ahead." I mused how one attribute of revival might well be, "Would these two very special little boys see a difference in me?" What were the dinosaurs? They were memories. While I may never know if their young hearts sensed Jesus in me, well over a year later while recuperating from a traumatic hospitalization of my own, I received crayon-drawn art work in the mail. Yes, it was from these two young boys (of course, mailed by their mother). It was exactly what I needed that day to bring a little light into a heavy moment in my life. Here they were now ministering to me. To be in your children's lives tomorrow, you have to be in their lives today. Maybe that's where revival begins. I don't want to go to a revival. I want to be a revival.

> *I mused how one attribute of revival might well be, "Would these two very special little boys see a difference in me?"*

Is revival possible for our generation? Societal plights may appear irreparable unless God intervenes. It's as if we live in a Jurassic land: monstrous creatures awaiting supremacy over anything humane or decent. Abortion has for decades now become mainstream and simply accepted. Add to it racism, sexual promiscuity and diseases from such behaviors, infidelity, betrayal, deceit, unnatural affections, complacency, political and partisan battles, radicalism, martyrdom, rampant inequalities, and silence from the Church. Most of these things are not new but the result of centuries—even millennia—of spiritual and moral decline.

Through divine love, the Trinity, leading the Son to death, burial, and resurrection, identified His slaying on the Cross—and His living again—as paramount in God's saving and redeeming grace. From this one moment, God has revived generations and movements to reestablish and restore sacred truth and by such, to transform the Church.

I am reminded that where I started my life and journey does not determine where I end up. It works the same for you and for those you minister to. Every advantage can be offered to young lives, prosperity, affluence, you name it. Those gifts can still be wasted and nothing of value be captured. Likewise, you can begin with nothing and become successful in all you do. It depends on you. Attitude is far more significant than race, gender, or one's perception or presumption of their social class.

In light of these things, we must ask ourselves, "Is it possible that *I* could have a role in the revival of the modern Church?" If revival has a personal element, I came to wonder if these little boys saw Jesus in me.

"'Son of man, can these bones live?'
God asked the prophet Ezekiel"
(Ezekiel 37:3, NIV).

Chapter 2

Revival at Cane Ridge, Paris, KY (1801)

"Will you not revive us again, that your people may rejoice in you?"
(Psalm 85:6, ESV).

On September 11, 2001 (also referred to as 9/11), I was traveling scenic roads and admiring the beauty of Kentucky horse farms en route to Paris, Kentucky's Cane Ridge camp meeting site. The sun bearing down on Kentucky horse farms on a crisp and clear autumn morning in the Bluegrass brings one a feeling few other places can provide. The famous revival site is only one hour and forty-five minutes' driving time from my home in a Louisville suburb. It was to be my first visit to Cane Ridge. Don Moen, an international singer and worship leader then associated with Hosanna Integrity Music, was leading a regional prayer event.

At 8:46 a.m. Eastern Time, American Airlines Flight 11, the first of two commercial airplanes, crashed into the North Tower of New York City's famous twin towers. Al Qaeda terrorists, having hijacked four planes earlier in the morning, coordinated suicide flights against New York City's World Trade Center and Washington DC's Pentagon. In Pennsylvania, moments before all passengers would die, brave souls wrestled terrorist pilots until their plane crashed in an open field. Nearly 3,000 innocents lost their lives that day. A news alert came over my car radio announcing both towers falling within minutes of one another. The prayer meeting that morning was unlike any I have ever attended. It became clear and relevant that America needed God's touch, healing, and ever-present help in time of trouble. The rest is history.

> *Nearly 3,000 innocents lost their lives that day.*

America's need for God's touch and healing has been evident throughout its troubling history as European settlers striving to establish a new country clashed with Native Americans, perpetuated injustices of slavery and racism, and engaged in imminent civil unrest and war.

In the pages to follow, I will introduce the reader to one of the landmark events of the Second Great Awakening that began in Britain in the 1790s but quickly spread to the new United States. This quick read will in part address the history of revivals in context specific to the Cane Ridge Revival of 1801, its participants, and some key pastors and evangelists there. Additionally, discussion of strange manifestations that occurred during those few days of Kentucky revival often attributed to accounts of Cane Ridge, will give us a better understanding of the worshippers and searching souls and how they witnessed God's impact on their prayers.

> *Such a quest triggers us to partake in unpretentious revival that changes hearts and lives of our family members, friends, neighbors, and communities at large.*

I am privileged to live so closely to this historic holy site and have now visited it many times through the years. The revival crowds are long gone, and now only specially scheduled events are held there. Daily visitors are often just a few stragglers who found it by accident while touring nearby multi-million-dollar horse farms. Occasionally, revivalists—seekers who have specifically flown to visit there or who have driven out of their way—find this hidden gem.

In examining the account of revival we can absorb God's confirmation of restoring and transforming both the Church and culture, as we know it. We read of people and events in revival history that challenges us, awakens our spirits, drives our curiosities, and strengthens our faith. Such a quest triggers us to partake in unpretentious revival that changes hearts and lives of our family members, friends, neighbors, and communities at large.

Cane Ridge History
The Name and Location

The mid-eighteenth-century Great Awakening, often called the First Great Awakening (1730-1755), was attributed to names like Theodore Frelinghuysen, Jonathan Edwards, George Whitefield, and John Wesley.[1] By the later 1700s, however, those first revival fires had ceased in the Americas. Churches had become conformist and unproductive.

The Cane Ridge Revival was associated with the Second Awakening (1790-1840). Cane Ridge, Kentucky, is approximately a one-hour drive from Lexington, the second largest city in the Commonwealth of Kentucky, in what is now known as Paris, Kentucky.

To find Cane Ridge, one drives past numerous beautiful horse farms and scenic winding roads covered with the canopy of trees, green grass, and rolling hills. Several cities and towns in Kentucky have French origins: Paris, Versailles, Bellefonte, Bellevue, Frenchburg, LaGrange, LaFayette, Louisville (named in honor of King Louis XVI in 1778), to name a few. Paris, Kentucky, is in Bourbon County (also named with French origins in honor of the House of Bourbon, European Royal House), one of 120 counties in the Bluegrass State. Early American frontiersman, surveyor, explorer, and pioneer Daniel Boone likely named the smaller community of Cane Ridge. Boone's explorations throughout the region are numerous and well known, and I have stood at his gravesite where both he and his wife were buried in the state capital cemetery in Frankfort, Kentucky.

When you arrive to visit Cane Ridge today, you are greeted just outside the main entrance of the meeting house with remnants of cane bushes and bamboo still growing. Thus, the name Cane Ridge came to be known as the location where the great outpouring of God's Spirit took place during those days of the 1801 revival. It is probable that the bamboo stalks of cane covered acres of the land at the turn of the nineteenth century when the revival took place.

Allow me to offer as I begin, for those desiring to visit Cane Ridge or finding an appetite for more information about this American revival that saw tens of thousands in attendance, the physical address for this beautiful Kentucky drive: 1655 Cane Ridge Rd. (Highway 537), Paris, Kentucky. You can write the Cane Ridge curator at: P.O. Box 26, Paris, Kentucky 40362, call their listed number (859) 987-5350, review their website (www.caneridge.org), or email them at: curator@caneridge.org.

The Meeting House and Revival Grounds

Early Kentucky settlers and pioneers from Europe gravitated to the state's beautiful hillsides, freshwater streams, and fertile soil for their crops. In 1791, Scots-Irish Presbyterians settled the area and built Cane Ridge meeting house.[2] Settlers and enslaved people of African descent had also found their way to the farms of the Carolinas, Tennessee, Virginia, and Kentucky. The Cane Ridge Revival grounds were found to be an impeccable location for the new settlers. Shawnee and Cherokee Indians, Kentucky's most prominent Native Americans, had been driven from the land but not before great battles had taken hundreds of lives. Iain Murray writes, "As late as 1790, a Kentucky judge reported that in the previous seven years 'fifteen hundred souls had been killed or taken prisoner' by the Indians."[3]

Farms in this area were productive, towns were growing, and activity was abounding as the population steadily increased year to year. Military personnel at the time estimate "that some 20,000 to 30,000 persons of all ages, representing various cultures and economic levels traveled on foot and on horseback, many bringing wagons with tents and camping provisions" attended the revival.[4] For a crowd of this size to assemble and camp for several days, the revival grounds were found to be expansive and the fields open and readily conducive for such a gathering. With the grounds so large and the crowds so sizeable it was not uncommon for four to seven preachers to address the multitudes at the same time from various preaching points and stands that were erected as pulpits. Some stood on stumps or limbs of cut down trees while others stood on man-made platforms. Some stood in the shade while others were in the scorching August Kentucky heat.

On Friday, August 6, 1801, people began arriving at Cane Ridge for the first service to be held that evening in the meeting house. Rev. Matthew Houston was a colleague of Barton Stone. Stone was the pastor/revivalist at the time of the Cane Ridge revival. Houston offered the opening sermon.[5] Newell Williams acknowledged in his biography of Stone, "Sunday the day reserved for the celebration of the sacrament, was marked by a steady, pouring rain."[6] Though attendance estimates for the following week range from the aforementioned 20,000-30,000 people, "the number who attended was remarkable in a state with a recorded total population in 1800 of 220,095."[7] "No more than one hundred could be seated in the meeting house at one time," so Presbyterian ministers served Communion on a rotating basis to the hundreds who came inside to receive.[8] Not all Presbyterian ministers were excited about uniting the Communion service with Baptists and Methodists. Some of Stone's own elders at the Cane Ridge church expressed strong disapproval. Still, revival had come, and the sign of thousands hungering for Christ was obvious to all.

Now, over two centuries later, the church building built on the revival site has been enclosed under a large structure covering the entirety of the historic edifice for preservation purposes. The original construction remains intact and "is believed to be the largest one-room log structure standing in North America."[9]

Bathed in Prayer

Just over one hundred years prior to the great Azusa Street Revival, Kentucky found herself host to an outpouring of the Holy Spirit that unified saints and sinners, multiple churches and denominations, and those of mixed races, languages, and socio-economic backgrounds.

Every great revival has been bathed in prayer, and Cane Ridge was no exception. It was a united effort. Revival fires had begun to burn again amidst alarming atheism, agnosticism, and moral decline following the American Revolution. S. B. Shaw wrote of the Great Welsh Revival that Evan Roberts had prayed for thirteen months to come, spending hours praying and preaching until it was observed that the dominant note of the revival was prayer and praise.[10] Dan Graves writes, "Recognizing that many people on the Western frontier were indifferent to faith or actively opposed to it, pastors and Christians began to set aside time for prayer that revival might come."[11] Ten years of prayer meetings and Bible preaching at Cane Ridge preceded the Kentucky Revival. It was then that this building and the acres of land surrounding it hosted the revival outpouring of the Holy Spirit known as the Cane Ridge Revival in August 1801.

> *Kentucky found herself host to an outpouring of the Holy Spirit that unified saints and sinners, multiple churches and denominations, and those of mixed races, languages, and socio-economic backgrounds.*

The events of 1800-1801 in Kentucky "first began in individuals who had been under deep convictions of sin, and great trouble about their souls, and had fasted and prayed, and diligently searched the scriptures."[12] As Leonard Ravenhill writes, "Prayer is not a preparation for the battle; it is the battle!"[13] A spiritual battle ensued for the souls of men and women, young and old, black and white, rich and poor.

The power of God made manifest in the Cane Ridge meetings surprised both ministers and attendees alike. The meeting extended one full week and "was kept up by night and day."[14] Kentucky Presbyterian minister, David Rice, preached of the great revival, "The songs of the drunkard are exchanged for the songs of Zion; fervent prayer succeeds in the room of profane oaths and curses; the lying tongue has learned to speak truth in the fear of God, and the contentious firebrand is converted into a lover of peace."[15] Their preaching carried a confident theme: to be almost saved was to be totally lost. Decades following the Cane Ridge revival an English Particular Baptist preacher named Charles Haddon Spurgeon taught of a godless world being a lawless one where anarchy comes when the fear of God is forgotten.

With extreme manifestations of the revival, "some were offended and withdrew from the assembly, determined to oppose it as a work of the wicked one, but all their objections only ... tended ... the subjects of it to set out with warmer zeal to promote it."[16]

Additionally, "many fervent prayers were offered up in the revival for the poor Indians (of the region)."[17] Months or years later, many of the Indians joined the Kentucky Shakers movement,[18] which settled near Wilmore, Kentucky, now home of Asbury Theological Seminary and Asbury University. Today, the Shaker Village features a wonderful historic tour of the farm, acres, existing buildings still standing, and restaurants filled daily with tourists arriving to enjoy the entirety of the meal grown on the present Shaker farm.

Cane Ridge Participants
Introduction

Most churches across the United States today find individuals from numerous denominational or spiritual backgrounds attending their services. Some researchers have alluded that the 21st century American church has become a melting pot for those of varying spiritual experiences, doctrines, dogmas, and theologies. That was not the normative for colonial North America.

"The greatest number of professors [those attending the Kentucky Revival] might be ranked among the Presbyterians, Baptists, and Methodists ... acknowledging each other as sisters; yet standing entirely separate as to any communion or fellowship, and often treating one-another with the highest marks of hostility."[19] With the outpouring of the Holy Spirit to occur at Cane Ridge, at least for a season of this revival, separatist denominationalism was to change and unity unlike any previously seen among the ranks was to be witnessed among the thousands gathering for services and Communion. Unity was to be momentary. In time, "these excesses of the Kentucky revival divided churches and whole denominations, but the more extreme elements drew off into the Stonites (named after Barton Stone) which slid into the sect known as the Shakers, a self-explanatory title."[20] You will read later in this book of other revival flames that likewise found division and their embers burning out.

Of the egalitarian nature of the revival, Newell Williams writes, "Literally hundreds of persons exhorted at Cane Ridge; not only men, but women and even children. Observers marveled at the knowledge, eloquence, and depth of feeling communicated by persons not at all accustomed to preaching."[21] I am reminded of the first time I heard my daughter preach to a large crowd -on that occasion- of nearly 1500. She was anointed, engaged, well spoken, and clearly directed by the Lord. Within the last month of this writing, I sat in a local church service and heard a gentleman minister who admitted it was his first time to speak from behind the pulpit. He meaningfully shared God's word. God will use you, friend. I encourage you to let him.

By the end of the week, attendees of the Cane Ridge Revival had no choice but to begin long journeys home. "The meeting would have continued even longer had provisions in the neighborhood not been exhausted."[22] Yet the spiritual benefits reverberated: "The powerful work of the Spirit that swept across Kentucky ... left the state entirely changed leaving the state as remarkable for sobriety as they had formerly been for dissoluteness and immorality."[23] This is unique in light of the

Revival at Cane Ridge, Paris, KY (1801)

fact that Bourbon County, the home of Paris and Cane Ridge, Kentucky, is now associated with Bourbon whiskey, and Kentucky is well known for the state's more than 40 craft breweries: Jim Beam, Maker's Mark, Buffalo Trace, Wild Turkey, Four Roses, Ancient Age, Woodford Reserve, and dozens of others.

Of several preachers and evangelists associated with preaching sermons, leading prayer meetings, singing songs, leading worship or open (welcoming to all) Communion services in one fashion or another, there were three key ministers associated with the Cane Ridge Revival: Barton Stone, John McGee, and James McGready.

Whether Native Americans, free or enslaved people of African descent, varying denominational fellowships participating in Communion simultaneously (not the church systems protocol of the day), local curiosity seekers, town drunkards and moral misfits, or local church faithful, these clergy welcomed all and changed the landscape of religion, faith, and theology for thousands hungering for the things of God. I pray for the day when today's Church will look the same. A brief description of each of their ministries is discussed. Additionally, concise insight will be offered as to the many strange manifestations attributed to this revival camp meeting, all of which were surprising to the ministers and the attendees alike. What some view as odd or extreme, others find life changing. It is relative to note that perspective matters little when one encounters the divine.

> *These clergy welcomed all and changed the landscape of religion, faith, and theology for thousands hungering for the things of God.*

Barton Stone

Barton W. Stone had strong Methodist, Presbyterian, and Christian Church connections, having served at one time as a professor of languages at a Methodist academy in Georgia. Stone had been deeply impacted by the ministry of the Presbyterian minister and evangelist James McGready (1763-1817), and in 1820 planted a Christian church in Georgetown, Kentucky, that grew to over two hundred members.[24] Stone, known to have been married at least three times,[25] had ten children.[26] He was quite ecumenical in his ministry journey, clearly more captivated in the work of the Lord than in where he preached it.

On July 2, 1801, just one month prior to the Great Revival, twenty-eight-year-old Stone, having traveled over two hundred miles west by horseback (a trip of at least six days) to Greenville, Kentucky, married Elizabeth Campbell, a Presbyterian.[27] Stone's itinerant preaching across Kentucky had brought him to a number of pulpits and outstations where his fiery brand of preaching had stoked revival flames. It is apparent that Miss Campbell had struck his fancy.

Young Stone had become the pastor of Kentucky's Cane Ridge meeting house. The Lord was to use this minister in ways he could have never imagined at the time. Hints of revival had been stirring for the last several months as Baptists, Methodists, Christian churches, and Presbyterians each gathered together in unity for Communion services during various instances, a fact certainly uncommon for the day since each fellowship held distinctly different views on the Christian life and the sacraments.

Rev. Stone scheduled a Communion service during the first week of August 1801 and at the time had not yet disclosed his Methodist ties to his Presbyterian congregation of whom many were concerned as they realized his open Communion was to include Methodists and Baptists and others of all religious inclinations in the area.

I related well on a personal level to Stone's approach. In my early years, staunch Southern Baptist parents raised me. I then attended a primarily United Methodist seminary after undergraduate studies. Entering ministry, I credentialed with the Assemblies of God. Multiple friends and family are to date, Catholic, Episcopal, Independent, Lutheran, or one of multiple fellowships.

"Instead of the usual hundreds, thousands of people thronged toward Cane Ridge, hungering for a taste of God."[28] As mentioned above, many of Stone's followers gravitated to what became known as the Shakers, a movement identified by sometimes-extreme manifestations during worship and prayer.

Deeply impacted by the ministry of McGready, Stone once reported after hearing McGready preach that before the evangelist had finished speaking, Stone had lost all hope of having been converted, so deep was the conviction of sin upon his life.[29] Stone's mother, who later became a Methodist, was converted during a visit home from her son. He had moments of depression from feeling lost and confused as to his spiritual state after McGready's preaching, and the visit home to see his mother was to encourage him.[30] Witnessing her son's darkened state, she herself sought the religious life and converted to a life of following Jesus Christ and His teachings. During this time, Stone heard a sermon titled, "God is Love," by Presbyterian minister William Hodge and was deeply moved; in that moment he felt complete in accepting his conversion and genuine salvation.[31]

> *Stone's mother, who later became a Methodist, was converted during a visit home from her son.*

Frequently invited to social events while serving as a Methodist college professor in Georgia, Stone found his faith and personal devotions to God and the Church weakening and considered his attendance at such social functions "a snare."[32] He promptly started denying himself further these occasions "in order to live more devoted to God."[33]

John McGee

It is said of John McGee that "men filled their wagons with beds and provisions and traveled fifty miles to camp upon the ground and hear him preach."[34] McGee's preaching style was beyond the customary refinements and Bible preaching. "The Methodist preacher ... after a brief debate in his own mind, came to the conclusion that it was his duty to disregard the usual orderly habits of the denomination, and passed along the aisles shouting and exhorting vehemently."[35] Stone had admitted that the numbers of individuals falling to the ground during services as if they were dead was a new and strange phenomenon to him. While the number of persons falling was unusual, numerous accounts of individuals falling had been associated with the eighteenth-century revivals of John Wesley in England and of Jonathan Edwards and George Whitefield in America. It is probably no coincidence, knowing the ministry style of John McGee, that the first report of a person falling in the Great Revival occurred in response to the efforts of this Methodist evangelist.[36] As Paul Conkin notes, "The role of John McGee gave the Methodists special claim to the great revival."[37] His preaching style followed typical era "Methodist fashion exhorting from the heart, moving in tears and with frequent shouts through the congregation."[38] One could only imagine the numbers of Cane Ridge revival preachers who imitated his style.

James McGready

While Barton Stone remains the influential character of the Cane Ridge Revival, he had clearly been influenced in camp meetings previously by other area-renowned preachers. In 1800, a year before the Cane Ridge Revival, revival began in Kentucky under the exhortations of a fiery Presbyterian preacher named James McGready in Logan County.[39] This is often considered the first camp meeting in the United States. Logan County is approximately 225 miles west from Paris and the Cane Ridge camp meeting site. Several smaller revivals spread from that ministry, but the great revival of Cane Ridge was yet to occur. In those days of primitive horse-drawn carriage or horseback the trip from Logan County to Cane Ridge would have been nearly a two-week wagon journey for most families. The dedication of hungry revivalists was evidence of the drawing of the Holy Spirit upon their hearts.

McGready, a Presbyterian minister, was known for his fiery preaching on God's wrath. Not unlike many of the Bible prophets, he had fled for his life after previous campaigns. Once such, in North Carolina, because of the enraged crowds. He had received a grammar school education in western Pennsylvania but forsook opportunities for comfortable ministry there to pastor three small churches – a three-point charge - in Logan County, Kentucky. His messages, "judging from his published sermons, focused on the pursuit of happiness,"[40] which was not to be found in physical pleasures or wealth and possessions but rather in knowledge and relationship with God. "He touched people by his prayers and sermons, and at the same time troubled them by his denunciations of anything less than perfect holiness in conduct."[41] Evangelistically, McGready often concluded his sermons "with a call to sinners to flee the wrath to come without delay."[42] Rev. McGready ministered to three rural congregations: Gasper River, Muddy River, and Red River. In this season, few churches were found throughout the whole of Kentucky. There were towns where worship services had never been conducted. The common rule of order was most often that of no order at all. Kentucky at large and the areas around Logan County most especially were spiritually barren and challenging in every way.

> *Evangelistically, McGready often concluded his sermons "with a call to sinners to flee the wrath to come without delay."*

That said, the revival services held by McGready were marked by far more than his powerful messages. The reverend would have people praying for him at sunset every Saturday and sunrise every Sunday. Further, his congregants held concerts of prayer at least once each month. As success in the meetings grew, the pastor sent promotional materials and notices weeks in advance announcing sacramental services to be offered. Wagons and horses from a hundred miles came expectantly waiting on God's touch for their lives and families. Wagon trains delivered tents, bedrolls, and every expected necessity. McGready's preaching with brilliant expressions of heaven and hell had an influential impact on Barton Stone. Detailed accounts of this revivalist's theology and doctrinal preaching are offered in D.

Newell William's book, *Barton Stone: A Spiritual Biography*. The McGready revivals of Red River and Gasper River challenged Stone in such a way that a second revival soon followed at Cane Ridge in August 1801. This one raced across the western frontier and was not reliant on location or ambiance but rather followed praying saints and penitent sinners. Thousands were converted at Cane Ridge; notably, one Peter Cartwright, who it is said personally baptized over twelve thousand converts and was later elected to the Illinois legislature. His hatred of the sin of slavery in Kentucky ultimately convinced him to move to Illinois where slavery was illegal.

Cane Ridge Strange Manifestations
Jerks, Revival Signs, and Controversies

Those who attended the Cane Ridge meetings witnessed numerous signs and wonders. Before we go too much further allow me to offer a few simple insights about such extremes. Today's church needs accountability. Ministers must guard themselves from ploys to topple integrity and spiritual fervor. Burn-out, failures, and disillusionment can set in when spiritual coverings are not in place. Don't forget that all your failures are erased. God washes away all your sin. God's shed blood makes you whole – again. A friend and life-long missionary to India, David Grant said, "Do not be skittish of the miraculous that the Lord would want to do in our lives just because others have crashed and burned." Jesus is still leading His church forward. Too often individuals miss the miraculous because of the experiences of others. When God is speaking to you, listen.

When Cane Ridge Revival services would be dismissed, the congregation showed no temperament to leave, many of them remaining quietly weeping in many parts of the meeting house. Others sat quivering under a mindfulness of the power of God. Preachers felt overpowering urges to preach, and the people were enthusiastic to listen. Women and men shouted, and emotions brought voices to the highest pitch. Uproar and bewilderment

Revival at Cane Ridge, Paris, KY (1801)

increased, and shrieks for mercy were blended with shouts of joyous delight and pure bliss.

As meetings continued, the excitement and anticipation of the crowds grew larger. Five, six, seven, or more preachers would all be preaching simultaneously. Groups of eight, nine, or ten people would be encircled singing hymns. Then, suddenly a preacher would step upon a chopped down tree stump and begin zealously exhorting from God's Word. The people would rush "from preacher to preacher, singing, shouting, laughing, and calling men and women to repent."[43] In frenzied worship or upon the listening to God's Word many would fall to the ground unable to get up, often appearing lifeless or in a controlled state of mind. Those who fell were gathered up and carried to the meeting house, where those slain in the Spirit, as it were called, were laid upon the floor.[44] When reading of Scotland's Lewis Awakening, Campbell wrote of people falling to the ground in services led by George Whitefield, saying to not remove them from the sanctuary, as had been the normalcy, but rather, "Don't be wiser than God. Let them cry out; it will do a great deal more good than your preaching."[45] Do you remember what my friend, David Grant had said? David has preached to thousands across India and the nations. He's seen a thing or two in the spiritual realm that many miss because they're too quick to dismiss something and neglect what God might want to do. It remains imperative today that we allow room and time for the Holy Spirit to lead church services rather than man's agendas or pre-set service schedules. If hungering individuals are willing clergy must allow them to linger in God's presence, which is far more powerful than the best attempts of men's sermons.

Peter Cartwright wrote in *Autobiography of Peter Cartwright: The Backwoods Preacher*, that several "members ran wild and indulged in some extravagancies that were hard to control ... Many were seized with convulsive jerking all over, which they could not by any possibility avoid, and the more they resisted the more they jerked."[46] Several accounts reported of congregants and attendees at Cane Ridge weeping, some shouting, and many (thousands) being converted. Once wild, cursing, gamblers, drunkards, and spiritually bankrupt frontiersmen were now to form caravans moving north, south, east, and west proclaiming a beforehand unknown and most genuine Christian faith. Other strange and wild exercises befalling revival crowds included running, jumping, and a most extreme barking exercise that overcame some of the faithful. "Others were moved by a voluntary exercise of dancing ... leaping ... or skipping."[47]

> Among the most remarkable of these cases ... were those in the Kentucky revival ... and accounts given by physicians who were eye-witnesses ... of ... the jerks with violent spasmodic contractions of the muscles ... head turning quickly right to left ... throwing persons on the ground where they would roll about strangely.[48]

The jerks, as they were called, seemed to affect with most distress those who were careless to revival. "It does not affect ... naturalists ... and rarely those who are the most pious; but the lukewarm ... and the persecutors are more subject to it than any, and they have sometimes cursed and swore and damned it, while jerking."[49] One man was reported to have jerked so violently back and forth, whiskey in hand and swearing on his lips throughout the episode, until he snapped his neck, fell, and soon died on the revival grounds.

Prophecy and predictions of end time events was also not uncommon.

Many professed to "fall into trances and see visions; they would fall at meetings and sometimes at home, and lay apparently powerless and motionless for days, sometimes for a week at a time, without food or drink."[50] When they awakened, they declared having seen heaven and hell, and God, angels, the devil and the damned. Prophecy and predictions of end time events was also not uncommon.

Regarding these phenomena, "John Wesley looked upon these physical agitations as proofs of the divine presence. Charles Wesley suspected and discouraged them. Whitfield was incredulous. Edwards puts in an apology for them. But very few ministers favored them."[51] Nevertheless, the Kentucky Revival "preaching was direct and pungent, and aimed at the immediate conversion of sinners ... and promoted by similar efforts of the different denominations united."[52] Though separate in their pre-revival standard communion, each of the denominational groups present found themselves in unity and harmony in their desire for salvation of sinners and the spiritual renewal of saints.

"In the months to follow the great revival, Baptist Associations soon had difficulties ... Methodists seem to have been largely unaffected for reasons yet noted ... and Presbyterians were virtually shattered by divisions."[53] Of the ministers participating in the revival,

> ... one Presbyterian became a Quaker, another took his people into union with Alexander Campbell's Disciples of Christ ... two others became Shakers ... and three formed the Cumberland Presbyterian Church, rejecting Calvinistic confession of faith.[54]

Likely, others did not like organized religion at all. There were no worries there. While divine moves of God must be pastored, they don't always seem that organized.

Conclusion

How does one know revival has broken out? Is it possible you are experiencing revival already in your midst and have yet to recognize it? Do not look to repeat something of the past. Do not try to imitate what the church down the street experienced. Cane Ridge, the Red River Revival, Brownsville, Toronto, and Azusa all took their place in God's work. This time our Father plans that which has not been seen before.

> May we be reminded, "No eye has seen, no ear has heard, no mind has conceived what God has prepared for those who love him." (I Cor. 2:9 NIV)

Is it the large audiences attracted, such as with twentieth-century Billy Graham crusades or the thousands that encamped on a Kentucky cane hill so many years ago? What does revival *mean*? According to *The Concise Dictionary of the Christian Tradition*, revival is "A tremendous outpouring of the Holy

Spirit on a church or churches in a specific area. The results are felt both in terms of the internal life of the people and in their mission to the world."[55] This revival sparked a missionary movement around the globe. Hundreds of colleges were begun in the short years to follow by these revival attendees. The Church had once again impacted the world. Frontier revelry was replaced with honesty and integrity, a decrease in crime, and a season of national prosperity to follow.

Many have never read or as much as heard of the Cane Ridge Revival meetings of August 1801. Throughout this synopsis of the revival, I have addressed historical perspective, the key evangelists of the events, and numerous strange manifestations associated with this encounter from God—all new and foreign to early Kentucky settlers and pioneers of the day. It very well could be foreign to, our reader, as well.

Reviewing the history of this revival, the reader comes to appreciate a broader lens of the geographical location of the great event and a better understanding of why the settlers called it Cane Ridge. Further historical narrative discusses the meeting house itself and the numerous acres of revival grounds where this outpouring occurred. As all revivals have witnessed, this work acknowledges the power of prayer and its impact on this divine encounter with God at Cane Ridge, Kentucky. Revival does not simply occur on its own. It results from worshipping hearts interceding faithfully for truth—God's truth. The devil wants you to pay attention to your feelings. Jesus wants you to pay attention to His truth.

> *Revival does not simply occur on its own. It results from worshipping hearts interceding faithfully for truth—God's truth.*

We also catch a glimpse of those in this awakening who were not enthused with the idea of these revivalists offering open communion to such divergent audiences. We detect how this large gathering, though a spiritual awakening within itself, drew crowds of onlookers, skeptical observers, and faint participants.

Revival at Cane Ridge, Paris, KY (1801)

We observe the many challenges these Cane Ridge attendees faced in trying to maintain an ongoing revival. And, we ponder how these things might play out today in a sovereign move of God upon the church or our nations?

It is my hope in bringing again the amazing history of Kentucky's Cane Ridge Revival to our remembrance that those who are searching will seek and meet the same God who changed the landscape of America's Midwest at the turn of the nineteenth century. For revivalists today and those drawn to a deeper encounter in faith, it bodes well to be reminded that the God of Cane Ridge, the God of the First and Second Great Awakenings, and the God of those calling out in faith in their last moments of life on an airplane spiraling on 9/11 after a terrorist attack, is the same yesterday, today, and forever. Take this moment and consider history. We may not always understand the supernatural, but I challenge you to a walk in faith with Jesus Christ as your Guide. Seek Him as fervently as they did, and see what He might provide or do in your life, as well. I've said before that the life of faith is lived in the deep end of the pool. Jump in. In the Gospel of Luke we read that Jesus went a short distance away from the others where He knelt down and prayed. Let me remind you that the final prayer of Jesus was about *you*.

> "As for you, the anointing you received from him
> remains in you, and you do not need anyone to teach you.
> But as his anointing teaches you about all things
> and as that anointing is real, not counterfeit—
> just as it has taught you, remain in him"
> (1 John 2:27, NIV).

Chapter 3

Revival at Asbury College, Wilmore, KY (1970)

"Create in me a clean heart, O God, and renew a right spirit within me"
(Psalm 51:10, ESV).

Introduction

Wherever sin and rebellion against God is found, so is exposed the necessity for revival. Human need for revival can be traced to the Fall. The most striking model of revival originates in the book of Acts. Jesus pledged to His disciples power through the Holy Spirit to personally witness of what was soon to occur—His death and resurrection. He gave specific instructions for them to take this good news to Jerusalem and across the earth. Some theorized they cast lots to determine who would travel to which part of the world to share the gospel.

In that spreading, the Church was established, and revival resulted from their evangelistic campaigns, though each met peril. Legends abound as to their demise: Andrew, Philip, Bartholomew, Peter, and James crucified; John, boiled in a pot of hot oil; Thomas speared; and Paul and Matthew beheaded. The fate for many other early followers was similar, and today, martyrdom continues for those challenged to stand against tyranny.

Are we willing like them to die for the Lord? That is the question of the centuries. I prefer to ask myself, "Am I willing to *live* for Him?"

At least four disciples were fishermen. Perhaps this is the reason for the earliest of Christian symbols, the fish? The Greek word for "fish," *ichthus*, formed an acrostic: *Iesous Christos Theou Uios Soter*, ("Jesus Christ, Son of God, Savior"). That symbol has continued throughout Church history. Just a few short miles from the Asbury campus in Kentucky, I used to trek annually with the church youth group I led in the late 1980s to the then regionally renowned, Icthus Christian Music Festival. The faith of thousands of young followers was stirred in those meetings that had begun on annual basis just months following the Asbury College Revival in 1970. Former Vice President of the United States, the Honorable Mike Pence, would later acknowledge his own spiritual awakening from a late-1970s visit to the same Icthus Music Festival in Wilmore, Kentucky.

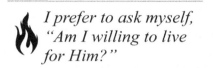

A few years prior to my own Icthus Festival outings, and fourteen years following the Asbury Revival of 1970, I entered Asbury Theological Seminary in 1984 to work on my masters degree. I had made, only two years earlier a genuine decision to live for Christ. The recent revival was not a prominent subject related to my classes, nor did professors, chapels, or other classmates address it during my time at the seminary to my recollection.

Years later, driving from my home in Louisville to Wilmore, Kentucky, for this research I was reminded of the serenity of Kentucky horse farms and the flowing bluegrass of the area.

John Wesley Hughes founded Asbury College in 1890. In 1928 he was asked to speak for the groundbreaking ceremony

Revival at Asbury College, Wilmore, KY (1970)

of what is still used today at this historic campus, Hughes Auditorium. I arrived to do research and stood that day in Hughes Chapel, the site of the campus chapel service on February 3, 1970 that lasted eight days before students again began trickling back to their classes. I knelt to momentarily pray at the nearly century-old worn and original, now aged beautifully preserved dark wooden altars at the front of this striking and hallowed hall.

As witnessed by cities ravaged again with racial chaos in recent weeks and America's generation's-old moral deficiencies evidenced by contemporary Supreme Court decisions that challenge biblical theology of same-sex marriage laws, among others, gives notice that our country desperately needs another move of God. America needs transformation within our society and the Church for holiness and redemptive power. God's Church has globally remained under siege for centuries. Yet, the increase in cultural rejection of Christian values and moments of the Church's own lethargy, apostasy, idolatry, and self-indulgences cannot prevent the fruit of generations of praying saints. The world is divided enough. It needs a united Church. Revival is breaking out across the nations, and the next wave of revival could come at any moment.

> Revival is breaking out across the nations, and the next wave of revival could come at any moment.

What does that mean? Do you remember us commenting that there have been generational cycles of the Holy Spirit's outpouring on societies? God continually and divinely interposes the habitual course of mortal affairs. Humanity's need for revival began with the Old Testament fall of man. Sin and rebellion against God leaves the need for revival, repentance, and renewal. In the Old Testament Israel would fall into sin. God would send prophets to warn the people and guide them to safety. When God's judgment would come the people would repent, revival would occur, God's blessings would abound, and the cycle would begin again. The Asbury revival was yet another continuation of the cycle in the life of 20th century North America. Over fifty years later today's western culture has accepted the excuse of people saying, "I was born this way". That's why Jesus said you must be born again. The 1970 Asbury College revival sent waves of repentance across the land bringing scores of new found converts and believers to the foot of the cross.

Upon arrival at the now Asbury University Library, I politely smiled as the young teenage college student working the front desk looked back at this fifties year old middle-aged man admitting she had never heard of the 1970 Asbury Revival. A gracious grin covered my disheartened awareness that forty-five years after this amazing encounter of God, students who sit weekly in the same chapel and walk on sidewalks within steps of one of the greatest revival encounters of the twentieth century have no idea of what God did here that cold wintry week in February 1970.

This chapter gives the reader an outside lens to the questions of what it may have been like to offer during those miraculous days of renewal and spiritual awakening. I will review both this revival's history and first-hand testimonials of the Asbury College Revival.

The Story
Asbury College Revival History

Asbury University today stands in Wesleyan theological tradition, holding that it is an action of God's grace by which one obtains the offer of salvation through the life, death, burial, and resurrection of Jesus Christ. Jesus can certainly change a human heart, and through His mercy that person can experience holiness, exhibit love, and become a representative of God's grace for the expansion of His kingdom on earth.

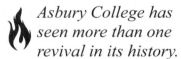
Asbury College has seen more than one revival in its history.

Asbury College has seen more than one revival in its history. Continued research uncovered numerous evidences of God reaching down from heaven to touch this campus, her students, local cities and towns, and the nation at large from this quiet

Kentucky community. Asbury College was established in 1890 and was named for Francis Asbury, the first Methodist bishop and circuit rider in the United States. Originally named Bethel Academy, it was the second Methodist school in the United States.[56] In 1790, Bishop Francis Asbury laid plans for Bethel Academy four miles southeast of Wilmore on the cliffs above the Kentucky River. It was operating by 1794 but closed in 1804 due to lack of funds and hostilities with local Indians.[57]

The dream continued, and the reestablishment of the school has indelibly touched the nation and the world. Numerous revival accounts have been renowned from the Asbury College campus in Wilmore, Kentucky. I will address several such occurrences.

The first was in blizzard weather of February 1905, when a prayer meeting in the men's dorm spilled out to the rest of the campus and into the town of Wilmore. This was fourteen months prior to another revival lasting nine years that marked the world: Azusa Street, Los Angeles.

A second Asbury revival came in February 1908, when a two-week revival broke out while prayers were being offered in the chapel. Prevailing prayer signified this move of God. Other revivals across the world were occurring at the same time. One was the Manchurian Revival (in what is now Liaoning Province, China), led by Presbyterian minister, Jonathan Goforth.

A third Asbury College revival event transpired in February 1921, when the prayers and worship of students extended the final service of a planned revival event lasting three days without breaking. England was experiencing revival at the same time. Douglas Brown, a Baptist minister in South London, was seeing untold conversions each Lord's Day. The Fisherman's Revival that crossed England and Scotland changed lives, marriages, filled meeting houses, and closed bars. Duncan Campbell of Scotland was leading the Hebrides Revival, transcending denominational boundaries and seeing crime nearly disappear in town after town after he would preach. It appears that Asbury College was seeing God's hand move at just the same time.

Fourthly, on February 23, 1950, Asbury College "became a center of activity and drew attention of this nation almost overnight"[58] when a student testimony led to confessions, intense prayer, and an uninterrupted revival for 118 hours. From this touch of God, it was estimated that 50,000 people nationwide found a new experience in Christ as a result of the revival and the witness teams that went out from it.[59] It was said that Central Bible Institute (now consolidated into Evangel University in Springfield, Missouri) had reported just days later, beginning on March 5, 1950, experiences of the deepest revival faculty members at the time could recall.

> *Those all-but-simple eight days led to six weeks of continued repentance and prayer, and over 2,000 witness teams traveling from Wilmore, Kentucky to churches and at least 130 college campuses around the United States.*

Further in the 1950s, evangelists including A. A. Allen, Kenneth Hagan, Oral Roberts, Jack Moore, T. L. Osborn, and William Branham led Charismatic and Pentecostalism to new heights in the American faith movement that became the Charismatic Renewal of the 1960s and beyond. Today, Pentecostalism is of the swiftest developing movements in Christendom crossing cultural and denominational impediments.

In March 1958, a fifth Asbury revival began in a season of student fasting and prayer meetings lasting 63 hours.

The 1970 Asbury Revival

Of primary importance for this study is the sixth Asbury revival, the revival of 1970, that occurred in another February visitation from God. On February 3, student confessions and testimonies led to (what some might say was "only") eight days of unbroken revival. Those all-but-simple eight days led to six weeks of continued repentance and prayer, and over 2,000 witness teams traveling from Wilmore, Kentucky to churches and at least 130

Revival at Asbury College, Wilmore, KY (1970)

college campuses around the United States.

On February 3, 1970, the scheduled speaker for Asbury's student chapel service was Custer Reynolds, academic dean and a Methodist layman. Asbury President Kinlaw was traveling to meetings in Canada at the time, so Dean Reynolds was in charge. Rather than preaching a sermon that day as expected and planned, Reynolds felt inclined to give a personal testimony of his own life, his spiritual journey, and his personal walk with God, inviting students to do the same. One student responded to testify. Then another student came to the microphone. Then more students stood and came forward to talk about their own experiences in Christ.[60] Soon the altar filled with students, broken, in tears, prayers, and repentance. Revival resulted.

That day, a chapel service to have lasted one hour continued into the afternoon and evening hours uninterrupted. It was soon to be tagged "a love-in"[61] with students finding enduring answers to troublesome problems. Classes also ceased at Asbury Theological Seminary, located directly across the street from the college. Hundreds of seminarians flocked to the Hughes Chapel auditorium to the Asbury College revival site. They were witnessing a divine impartation unlike anything they had ever seen before or would likely see thereafter.

Of the 1970 outpouring, Asbury College President at the time of the revival, Dr. Dennis Kinlaw, was quoted in *Christianity Today* saying, "God has taken the initiative. The revival is a student phenomenon ... and has given me a far greater sense of divine sovereignty."[62] Arthur Lindsay said, "An untold number of newspapers have either been on campus or contacted us by telephone for information. The Associated Press ... television and radio men have ...

> *I had only one thing on my mind; returning as soon as I could. I knew I was witnessing the divine presence of God.*

joined in the ministry of spreading news of God's great work here."[63] An editorial in the Wheeling, West Virginia *News Register*, February 8, 1970 by Don Daniels states, "The estimate was that possibl[y] 12,000 persons, many of them townspeople and many from a great distance, had heard the word and joined the throng."[64]

Subsequent Asbury Revivals

Recent years have also seen revival touch the Asbury community. In March 1992, the seventh Asbury revival began with student confessions during the closing chapel of the annual Holiness Conference. It turned into 127 hours of consecutive prayer and praise.

An eighth Asbury revival erupted in February 2006, as a student chapel led to four days of continuous worship, repentance, and prayer. Suzanne Gehring, former Asbury University Archive Librarian, was present during the 2006 outpouring. She recounts,

> I did not move from my seat from 10 o'clock in the morning until 5:00 o'clock in the evening. I was afraid to move or leave. I had a family at my home nearby and knew I had to get to them. I had only one thing on my mind; returning as soon as I could. I knew I was witnessing the divine presence of God.[65]

It is evident that fervent prayer accompanied each of the Asbury College revivals. Leonard Ravenhill writes, "Prayer is not a preparation for the battle; it is the battle! ... The more men pray, the less worldly they become. The less they pray, the more worldly they become. I am, of course, speaking of professing Christians at this point."[66] Asbury College, filled with Christian young men and women for over a century, has remained committed to prayer, worship, and a call to holiness, as evidenced by what I found when visiting this revival site. The beautiful Hughes Chapel auditorium is adorned with the statement emblazoned above the pipe organ at center stage, "Holiness Unto The Lord," which stood witness to the revival fires from the original wooden altar area below. Hughes Auditorium hymnbooks dating to the 1940s were evident in the chapel and well used.

The Impact: 1970 Asbury College Revival Testimonials

On Tuesday, February 24, 1970, twenty-one days after the beginning of this campus revival that went uninterrupted for eight days and nights, calls continued to come to the Asbury College public relations office for witness teams. As the Asbury archives note,

> The calls for students have completely broken down denominational barriers with Lutheran, Baptist, Nazarene, Methodist, Christian and Missionary Alliance, Church of God, Brethren, Mennonite, Church of Christ, Presbyterian, Episcopalian, and independent churches making invitations.[67]

Considering the testimonies from this revival, one must begin with the cornerstone of Hughes Auditorium, seen by all who begin the walk up the steps to the substantial and magnificent entry doors over which is engraved, "Follow Peace With All Men And Holiness Without Which No Man Shall See The Lord, Hebrews 12:14." This building keystone trumpets the first testament seen as students during past revivals arrived and departed the auditorium from their profound spiritual experiences.

Testimonials from students at this revival include that of James Davis, who said, "Prior to this revival my Christian life had been full of contradictions. ... From the onset of the revival, I was skeptical. ... After a three-day struggle, I went to the altar. I still do not know what it was, but whatever, it met my need completely."[68] Student Nancy Chadwell wrote, "'To God be the glory ... great things He has done!' So many times I have sung this song without fully realizing. ...

After I took my eyes off people and focused them on Christ, He was able to show me deeper things.

After I took my eyes off people and focused them on Christ, He was able to show me deeper things."[69] Another student, Debbie Meyer, said "I was confronted with the reality that the Spirit of

God was in our midst and that He seemed to have no intention of leaving for quite some time."[70] Another student had been working on a term paper the morning of February 3, 1970, and admittedly skipped the mandatory chapel service to arrive in class at 11:00 o'clock finding he was the only person there. Another student, Homer Pointer, arriving to Hughes Chapel, said, "I knelt at the altar. ... I learned to expect a miracle."[71] Janie Wiley said, "The Scripture ... more than any other during this revival is, 'Things which are impossible with men are possible with God.'"[72]

At the time of the 1970 revival, my former pastor, Ken Groen, was finishing his Master of Divinity at Asbury Seminary, directly across the street from the Asbury College campus. When I called him for a personal interview of his testimony from the revival, he said that upon arriving to the college auditorium, he found it "filled with over a thousand college students, faculty and even community members."[73] Groen continued:

> I was spellbound. Wave after wave of people flocked to the altars, as students and others, standing in long lines, went to the podium to testify of how God had convicted them of sin, of pride, of bitterness, of living a façade, [and they were] testifying of salvations, the infilling of the Holy Spirit, physical healings, reconciliations, and being called into the ministry.[74]

Norman Grubb in his book, *Continuous Revival*, writes of what he calls "the missing link ... the mouth-committal horizontally as the real proof of the genuineness of the heart-committal before God."[75] Grubb expresses the power of individuals testifying, as both one's duty and one's privilege, to the Savior Who redeems from sin and shame. He says that "Testimony to God's deliverance belongs to the whole Church. It involves some account of what the deliverance is from. It is also proof of our genuine repentance and genuine brokenness."[76] The Asbury College Revival of 1970 brought God's presence and conviction in such a way as to draw thousands to the depth of personal change and testimony to God's transforming power in their lives.

The Theology: The 1970 Asbury College Revival in Light of Revival Characteristics

Dr. Carolyn Tennant taught her doctoral classes at Assemblies of God Theological Seminary of nine characteristics of revival.[77] In this section, the Asbury College Revival of 1970 is considered in context to nine characteristics of revival listed below.

Table 1: A Consideration of the 1970 Asbury College Revival Characteristics

Nine Characteristics of Revival	Characteristic prominently associated with Asbury College Revival of 1970?
1. Occurred in times of moral decline	Yes
2. Began in the heart of a consecrated servant	Yes
3. Rested on the Word of God and its power	Yes
4. Resulted in a return to the worship of God	Yes
5. Witnessed the destruction of idols	Yes
6. Recorded separation from sin	Yes
7. Had people returning to obey God's laws	Yes
8. Experienced a restoration of joy and gladness	Yes
9. Was followed by a period of national prosperity	Yes, certainly a spiritual prosperity

Let's briefly speak to some of the characteristics of revival listed above.

Occurs in Time of Moral Decline

Revivals are said to follow a time of national moral decline. Once again we see here in generations past a regression of sacred spiritual mores and revival following. This renewal occurred at a time of national protests, free love, and strong and dividing sentiments over the Vietnam War, while a drug epidemic including the use of marijuana, LSD, and barbiturates ravaged our country. "In 1960, the first Playboy Club was built in Chicago, and in the January 19, 1970 issue of *Time* magazine, on two different pages were pictures of topless women. In January 1970, Jerome Bruner of Harvard University was advocating that school children be taught about animals as a way of understanding themselves. Martin Luther King had been assassinated in 1968 and American racial tensions were still divisive."[78] Another lens could say that our nation had become focused on individualistic capital ventures and risk-taking. It appeared the Church was taking a back seat to pluralistic and contemporary thinking. The Asbury revival arrived in perfect timing for the renewal of the Church. Some might say it arrived "for such a time as this."

> *Our nation had become focused on individualistic capital ventures and risk-taking. It appeared the Church was taking a back seat to pluralistic and contemporary thinking.*

> Do not think that because you are in the king's house you alone of all the Jews will escape. For if you remain silent at this time, relief and deliverance for the Jews will arise from another place, but you and your father's family will perish. And who knows but that you have come to royal position for such a time as this (Esth 4:13-14, NIV).

Begins with a Consecrated Servant

The revival is attributed to having been spontaneous and led by no one individual personality. Still, the move of God came at the discerning redirection by the Holy Spirit of the planned chapel service by the college Academic Dean, Chester Reynolds. His humble decision to forego his planned sermon to share his personal testimony and his opening the microphone with invitation for students to share their own testimonies changed the course of this chapel service and impacted thousands across the globe. Revival cannot be planned or scheduled. It is not a series of meetings added to the church's calendar in the annual calendar planning session. "True and genuine revival is solely the work of God which He reveals in His own ways, at His own time, and exclusively for His individual glory." When revival occurs, it is often described as miraculous. It takes place when God's people grasp that there is nothing they can do, manufacture, or spiritually develop that brings hope for today's world. Only in God can the revival, the miraculous, the unheard of, and the cultural marvel occur.

Revival hearts manifest God's holiness, righteousness, and authority. They are filled with spiritual fruit: His love, mercy, peace, joy, and grace. They are humbled in God's presence and repentant for their own sin and the world's sin. Because the Holy Spirit orchestrates it all, no one individual actually "leads" a revival. Yet, it is clear that God selects and raises up apostolic, prophetic, pastoral, and authentically five-fold leaders[79] who reflect His glory and the attributes of revival. While revival is wholly a work of God, He calls those listening and further invites each of us to participate. He does not desire to do His work alone. We are "the people of His pasture" (Ps 95:7, NIV). The Church is the body of Christ. As Paul encourages the Corinthian believers about laboring together in Christ, "Therefore, my beloved brothers, be steadfast, immovable, always abounding in the work of the Lord, knowing that in the Lord your labor is not in vain" (1 Cor 15:58, NIV). Truly, Dean Reynolds had a heart of a consecrated servant, and his labor was not in vain.

Rests on the Word of God

This revival sparked a voice of its own. The preaching of God's Word was not a paramount structure of this revival, but the Word of God was abounding through students' hearts, in songs, and with prayer. Through the hundreds of individuals streaming to the microphone, the Word of God flowed freely as they quoted and shared Scriptures of God's work in their lives. Evidenced by the hymnbooks mentioned previously and the testimonies of songs spontaneously rising from the crowd, a genuine return to the worship of God was evident through the entirety of the Asbury Revival. In the First and Second Great Awakenings students from Yale led the way. In the 1970s, students from Asbury were now doing the same. Yes, Yale, Harvard, Princeton, and Oxford were once known as beacons for Christianity and founded as Bible-declaring religious institutions. What happened?

Throughout an awakening, individuals are overcome with a consciousness of God's manifest presence. Over time, priorities and goals are altered. Spirit-led personal examination of hearts becomes rare and often non-existent. Societies give way to hindrances to loving and obeying God, His Word, and His precepts. For too many the Word is a book of information rather than transformation. Un-confessed sin sets in. Pride and apathy about saving the lost follows. I recently heard evangelist Martha Tennison preach, "Do not reject the message because of the position of the messenger." Superficiality through prayerlessness comes, and soon biblical illiteracy leads whole segments of society to a hardening of hearts. Their love for God waxes cold.

In light of such human frailties, the Lord asks, "Who is he who will devote himself to be close to me?" (Jer 30:21, NIV). David writes in a time of repentance, "Create in me a pure heart, O God, and renew a steadfast spirit within me. Restore to me the joy of your salvation and grant me a willing spirit, to sustain me" (Ps 51:10, 12, NIV).

Witnesses the Destruction of Idols

The destruction of idols and separation from sin as characteristics of historical revivals were witnessed at the 1970 outpouring as idols of the heart and as an absolute abandonment to God with deep conviction of sin pressed deeply on all in attendance. Prior to revival, conditions of the heart include weak, ineffective churches and societal structures. Hearts are callous and lacking passion. Individuals display indifference, rebellion, and spiritual blindness. Revival brings spiritual awakening. Jesus says in the Gospel of Luke, "I tell you ... if they keep quiet, the stones will cry out" (19:40, NIV).

Obedience of God's Laws

This abandonment to God and drawing to holiness had people connected to the 1970 Asbury Revival returning to obey God's laws and living for His glory. As Pastor Ken Groen recounts, "Joy and gladness were very evident at the revival as singing, though never led, would swell from among the audience. At night one could hear the crescendo of worship two or three blocks away from Hughes Auditorium."[80] Some have defined the revival as an added great awakening. Entire assemblies (churches) offered public repentance and renewed faith professions as news spread of this outpouring of God.

Followed by National Prosperity

Professor Tennant's ninth revival characteristic is that true revivals are followed by a period of national prosperity to some extent. To this characteristic, I am hesitant as to whether an assured national prosperity could be attributed specifically to this Asbury 1970 outpouring. "In fact, history shows that moral standards continued to decline thereafter. Inflation grew dramatically worse five years later."[81] Yet, the 1970s saw an end to the United States involvement in the Vietnam War, progress of civil rights activists, and women's movements achieving a number of their goals. An economic recession led to high interest rates and inflation, a shortage of imports, and Middle East tensions, but other changes were soon to come in pop culture, educational reform, and politics. The Charismatic Renewal was attaining prominence.

Robert Coleman, reflecting on the 1970 Asbury Revival, notes,

> All moments in history are not the same. Some loom large like Mount Everest, towering high above what surrounds them. One of these divine moments came on February 3, 1970 ... as a visitation occurred in Wilmore, Kentucky, a

small town near Lexington. ... It was as if the campus had been invaded by another Power.[82]

The Psalmist said, "I commune with my heart in the night; I meditate and search my spirit" (Ps 77:6 RSV). This Asbury Revival witnessed communing, meditating, and searching of the hearts of the repentant. At 11:10 p.m. on Tuesday night, February 3, prayers continued to be lifted by students and attendees for churches in desperate need of revival. Witness of the first evening's prayers included, "A lovely saxophone playing "Take My Hand Precious Lord," and the congregation joining in the singing with weeping among several people."[83]

This Asbury Revival witnessed communing, meditating, and searching of the hearts of the repentant.

Of numerous witnessing teams that left from the campus after only a few days of the revival, Azusa Pacific College near Los Angeles, California, was of the first of many schools to feel the impact of what was happening at Asbury College. A call to the campus in California from the Dean of Asbury informed colleagues there of "a moving of the Holy Spirit that had begun in unusual power that day at Asbury."[84] Azusa Pacific College decided to have an Asbury student flown to their campus. That night the Azusa faculty engaged in an all-night prayer meeting. Revival "broke out in terrific power" the next morning in the Azusa Pacific College chapel following the testimony of the visiting Asburian.[85]

Conclusion

What about the future? Evangelicalism has valued revival, but it must demand it for its own maintenance.[86] Be ready. As mentioned previously, the next wave of revival could come at any moment. Second Chronicles 7:14 says, "If my people which are called by my name, shall humble themselves and pray, and seek my face, and turn from their wicked ways, then will I hear from heaven and will forgive their sin and heal their land" (NIV).

I am convinced that the Church's greatest days are ahead.

Revival at Asbury College, Wilmore, KY (1970)

Wherever you are, whatever your situation, why not let this year – now – be your best year ever for winning souls, global outreach, seeing baptisms occur, and reaching as many as we can with the gospel. Surrender everything there is of you to Him. Everything. Kathryn Kuhlman is credited with saying that when she did that, for the first time she realized what it meant to have real power.

A personal drive to visit again the campuses of Asbury University and Asbury Seminary, and research in the Asbury University Library and Archives directly stirred my spirit. Reading multiple accounts of the testimonials and personal insights from attendees, reviewing archived videos and numerous articles since written, reading an Asbury D.Min. dissertation on the revival published at the time of the twenty-fifth anniversary of the momentous outpouring, interviewing those who had been present and impacted by the revival, and walking and praying during my visit to the Asbury campus caused me to again examine my own heart. I remembered times when the Holy Spirit had made himself known to me through experiences of revival in my own life. I searched my heart for ungodly attitudes and asked the Lord to reveal to me those hidden places of darkness that could be made light for His glory and pleasure.

The power of what occurs when the Holy Spirit touches and changes hungry hearts cannot be underestimated. I remember meeting the late German-born evangelist, Reinhard Bonnke, following his addressing a ministry leader's meeting just a few years before his death. A crowd filled the doorway as he was leaving the auditorium. I found myself face to face. We took a photo together. As I stood there shaking his hand and introducing myself, I distinctly remember his commanding presence and his eyes looking directly to my own. He had no pretense of looking around me, over me, or to whomever of seeming more importance might be awaiting his greeting. That simple gesture made me think it was no wonder God had used him to such extent. I wondered what he might be discerning and reading inside me. Godly leaders will discern imbalance. He had been a missionary and preached throughout the world and Africa (primarily) since the late 1960s. It has been estimated that over 79 million people came to Christ through his preaching campaigns. Interestingly, he lived 79 years, passing away in December of 2019. Bonnke is said to have preached that there is a great expectation for things to come. Is revival possible for this generation? I believe so. I am expecting it. Sometimes things don't work out in people's lives quite like they anticipated. Life is not always what was expected. Neither is death. Occasionally, roots have to be pulled up. Maybe it's because God is working on something better.

I am prompted to pursue that expectation. God has a plan. And, when things don't seem to work out as I might expect, I am confident in God's promises and that His plan will be right on time. For God's faithful followers it behooves you to lean on this truth. "As long as it is day, we must do the work of Him who sent me. Night is coming, when no one can work" (John 9:4, NIV). There is revival truth older than a thousand generations and promises beyond things yet to come. Revival is not a series of services or a special guest preaching with the most powerful delivery of the oracles of God. Revival is God ordained in every sense.

> *Revival is not a series of services or a special guest preaching with the most powerful delivery of the oracles of God. Revival is God ordained in every sense.*

While exact dates vary in accordance to a number of overlapping dynamics and as it were to relate to which research or historical author one may read, the Great Awakening (1726-56) had renowned preachers like Whitefield, Wesley, and Edwards. The Second Great Awakening (1776-1810) saw moves of God on college campuses and frontier camp meetings. Evangelists Finney, Baker, and Nettleton saw thousands come to Christ in early 1800s (1813-1846). D. L. Moody led the way for global ecumenicalism (1857-1895). Pentecostal and global revivals continued well into the 1900s with Azusa Street's William Seymour and England's Smith Wigglesworth. Wigglesworth, born in a small English village, never initiated a noteworthy movement in his career, but pointedly contributed to revivals of Pentecost. Miracles, signs, and wonders were routine in his assemblies. It has been said that he refused to read another book or article other than the Bible. Thousands were saved and multiple churches were planted through his ministries.

Thereafter, Billy Sunday (early National League baseball hero who became one of the most riveting evangelists of the early 1900's), R. A. Torrey (Yale University graduate who became a captivating evangelist and the second President of Moody Bible School), Duncan Campbell (Hebrides Revival of 1949), Katherine Kuhlman, and Amie Semple McPherson (as previously mentioned), became household names. Likewise in the mid-1900s, Oral Roberts and Charles Templeton filled tents and stadiums with multitudes coming to Christ. Though so many names could be added to a list of pastors, evangelists, and world changers, today one might think of names from recent decades to the present, such as Carlos Annacondia, Joel Osteen, T. D. Jakes, Joyce Meyer, Billy Graham, Franklin Graham, Rick Warren, Paul Crouch, Luis Palau, Jack Van Impe, Beth Moore, Reinhard Bonnke, Christine Caine, Kyle Idleman, Charles Stanley, Charles Swindoll, Katherine Kuhlman, Amie Semple McPherson, Haddon Robinson, John Stott, Marilyn Hickey, Jack Hayford, D. James Kennedy, Juanita Bynum, Warren Wiersbe, Tim Keller, Kay Arthur, and more. While you and anyone else creating a list of influential preachers would have varying names on your lists, one thing is certain of each: their devotion to the Lord and His work impacted thousands. Isaiah 61:1 (NIV) proclaims, "The Spirit of the Sovereign LORD is on me, because the LORD has anointed me to proclaim good news to the poor. He has sent me to bind up the brokenhearted, to proclaim freedom for the captives and release from darkness for the prisoners..." Thousands of lives are changed because of the powerful and faithful delivery of men and women of God through the ages.

Liberty from binding chains is found in the revival fire of the One who walks on water, speaks to seas, and roars like a lion. He carries healing in His wings—Jesus.

Chapter 4

Revival at King's Way Assembly, Versailles, KY (1997)

"Behold, I stand at the door and knock. If anyone hears my voice and opens the door, I will come in to him and eat with him, and he with me"
(Revelation 3:20, ESV).

Introduction

While an undeniable number of churches have experienced supernatural revival seasons and there could be hundreds, even thousands, of pastors from across the nations to offer similar historical story lines, having personally pastored a church experiencing a season of revival, I have chosen to offer an respective memoir of this specific experience at the Kentucky church I served from 1988 until 2004.

Simultaneous with this revival account, a sister church in a nearby county of the Commonwealth of Kentucky only fifteen miles from King's Way Assembly experienced a two-year season likewise where an inexplicable captivating presence of God permeated their services weekly.

Just over twenty years later (2018-2019), and only thirty-one miles away in Paris, Kentucky, another outpouring occurred. Hundreds from across America traveled to experience God's manifest presence.

Church leaders from every continent long to understand and maneuver such moments when their churches experience the Lord's visitation. In the pages ahead, I will examine only a few of the lessons learned, what seemed to instigate revival, insights as to what brought decline to revival, challenges of revival seasons, and how leaders handled revival. The only way to genuinely process the journey of experiencing revival in a local setting is to let faith arise.

> *The only way to genuinely process the journey of experiencing revival in a local setting is to let faith arise.*

History: The Relative Backdrop for This Chronicle

On June 5, 1988, my wife and I began a sixteen-year journey with a small rural congregation and a youth group of three. Even then we sensed there was something very special about this little Kentucky church. I had believed that Renee and I were headed toward career global missions. I may not have ended up where I intended to go, but I do believe I landed where I needed to be. Maybe you've wondered the same about your life's trajectory. I can assure you that the Lord directs His children. Trust His plan for your life. He is faithful.

The Sunday morning worship at this church consisted of three hymns from a dated hymnal, led by a precious elder saint, and an overall honorable commitment of approximate annual missions giving leaning toward what I believed to be a humble $10,000.00.

My hand-written journal dated December 19, 1988 says, "Lord, I know you will work everything out. Please, bless my ministry here ... and allow me to see souls saved and a vision birthed for evangelism; also, please help the people enter into worship and heal broken wounds from problems past. You can do all things!"[87]

During a heartbroken moment in 1971, seven-time Grammy Award winning Andraé Crouch wrote a song that he titled, "Through It All." His lyrics wrote of having tears and sorrows, questions of his tomorrows, and times he didn't know what was right or wrong. Somehow through it all he still knew God would see him through.

I find comfort in that story. Many of us have found that promise true. Renee and I were just over six months into this new journey of serving on the small staff of this church when I was already seeing hurts, sensing discouragement, and believing for God's miraculous touch to see us through. Only years later did I read the amazing ministry works of David Brainerd, an early 1700's American missionary to the Native Americans. He wrote the essence of a prayer I prayed often during those ministry years. "Let me make a difference, Lord. Help me to do something (as Brainerd said) "utterly disproportionate to who I am."

We initially served as the first full-time associate and youth pastor hired in ministry for the fifty-year congregation. Our responsibilities were to lead and oversee music and youth ministries. The pastor's daughters who were not so fond of their new youth pastors would soon challenge me. Within eighteen months the pastor resigned under particular duress, and I was called to be the interim pastor during their pastoral search. Oddly, I had actually dreamt I was supposed to be the pastor. I chose not to act on that initially and told no one until long later. I want to be led by my dreams, not pressed by difficulties. Within months a new pastor had been selected. He was a charismatic leader, orator, and some might say quite a head-turner in a number of ways. He was my friend, prior, during the stress, and following his tenure—albeit strained at that juncture. Two years following being called to pastor the church, his

> *I may not have ended up where I intended to go, but I do believe I landed where I needed to be.*

personal life and ultimate marriage-ending divorce led to imminent resignation. I was serving a second time in four years as the interim pastor.

On September 6, 1992, Renee and I were elected as the lead pastors of the church, which at the time met in a local middle-school auditorium. We had only Sunday morning and Sunday evening services with no weekly classes or meetings, endured the weekly "set up and break down" of equipment for the service (so many of you reading this are rolling your eyes as you know exactly what I'm talking about having done it yourselves, no doubt), had very little money or church income, and through a most difficult transition of our previous pastor had dwindled from approximately 150 in actual weekly attendance to only 70-90 individuals—including the children and nursery.

The year to follow was a whirlwind of activity, outreach, and vision casting. It was a good season for Renee and me. We had a new baby born in November of 1991, and life was good. I mostly remember praying, seemingly begging God (whether right or wrong) that He would come and do only what He could do in our humble church family and situation. On Monday, September 27, 1993, in a one-year anniversary of our becoming pastors, the church had moved from the local school. We relocated to nearly forty prime acres (Phase 1 of our envisioned development and a small facility that would later become the fellowship hall of a new church we hoped would come soon). I found myself ready to lead the people to their, if you will, 'promised land.' Let me remind you, in such seasons, God is sovereignly in control, while we as leaders often stumble through pastoring the revival. In one year, with remarkable leaders from our initially humble and small group, we found the Lord faithful as He helped us design, start, organize, coordinate, and complete the first phase of construction. We simultaneously focused on missions and outreach, worship, and disciple making. I knew that *wearing* a cross on a gold chain (which I had worn and do to this day since a radical experience with the Lord in my university years) would not make me a disciple. I realized that *carrying* my cross would. What would that look like over the years to come?

Revival at King's Way Assembly Versailles, KY (1997)

I remember as a small boy following my dad through the snow. I can't remember when or where, but I do remember stretching each step to land where he had stepped before. Just to follow in those prints in the snow would be the safest place to walk.

My parents had divorced when I was a small boy. After three or four years of living in an all-guy household with my father and older brother, at ten years of age my dad remarried. My stepmother, Jessie, became "Mom" to me in every since of the way. She exemplified all that was good in my life. She lived humbly, and in joy, hope, kindness, empathy, and truth.

Her father, my grandfather (actually, he was my stepgrandfather), Bradley Chandler had married her mother when she was only 14 years old (as I remember being told the story). Her mother, Fannie Chandler, -to some extent- was from an American Indian (Native American) heritage (Cherokee, I believe). They served God, loved their large family, and worked hard on their farmland. They had their challenges, as do every family, but remained faithful to one-another and to God. That's a foundation of revival; remaining faithful to the God of the universe.

I heard it said once that an old Cherokee had told his grandson, "My son, there is a battle between two wolves inside us all. One is evil. It is anger, jealousy, greed, resentment, inferiority, lies, and ego. The other is good. It is joy, peace, love, hope, humility, kindness, empathy, and truth." The boy thought for a moment and asked, "Grandfather, which wolf wins?" The wrinkled and whiskered man of grey hair quietly looked lovingly at this grandson and responded, "The one you feed, my son."

Returning back to my story, my mother taught me to feed the latter; the good. At the time, I wasn't so sure I understood her lessons. Other kids would eat candy or a soda for breakfast. I would eat cereal, eggs and toast. Others would eat junk food for lunch. I would eat home-cooked meals. She wanted to know every friend, every location I would go, and what time I would be back at home each evening. I remember one event when on a date with a young lady from my high school. I had stayed far longer than I should have at the girl's home. At midnight that night my father (who did not know the girl or her parents) found the address of her home. He drove to the location, knocked on the door, and politely asked her mother if he could speak to his son. I went to the door to the surprise of seeing my father standing there at midnight that evening. He didn't yell. He didn't make a scene. He didn't embarrass me in any way. He simply said, "Son, this is wrong. You will come home now." I did. Nothing more was said about that incident. I learned my lesson. And, I never went out with that girl again.

My mom made me work in our one-acre garden, hoeing and raking row by row. I was the grounds keeper also. We also had a large yard for our home. I mowed another one-acre of grass weekly (with a push mower, of course). And, yes, she expected me to hand-rake, bag, and discard the grass if the mowed clippings were too thick after the exhausting event each week. She had me washing dirty dishes (my own), taught me to put things away immediately after using them, had me using the vacuum on the carpets, and making my bed each morning before I left for school and every day during our summer breaks. I was not allowed to eat in my bedroom. She taught me to iron my clothes, do the laundry, and make my bed. Yes, she would actually flip a coin on my bed spread (bed-cover) and if it crinkled or wrinkled, she would tell me it wasn't tight enough and I'd be asked to make it again. She insisted I tell the truth and always asked that I strive for "more", not accepting average in the daily routines. I saw them praying at every meal and reading their bible regularly. She wanted me to have opinions and wanted to know them. She and my dad had me in church almost every time their local church doors were open.

Some might say it seemed cruel. At almost sixty years old, I've never been arrested. I've never vandalized public or another's personal property. I have learned to respect other people's opinions especially when they don't match mine. And, other than a few speeding tickets (oops; sorry), I've never been in any trouble. My parents were God-fearing, honest, and hard working. That is a picture of discipleship. Too many individuals have made discipleship a packaged program, a Sunday School hour, or a Small Group bible study. Today's local church needs more people of towels and humility and fewer people scurrying for their seat at the head table. My mother and father exemplified that to me. My dad passed away in 2004, but I kept one pair of his shoes. They remain in my closet today as a reminder of the man I followed, where I came from, and the hope that I could follow to some degree in his footsteps.

My journal read on Monday morning following the first service (only one year after being elected pastor) in the new facility,

> Yesterday was our first service in the new building ... 305 in attendance ... I gave an altar call after a twenty-five-minute message ... altars filled ... D. H. was weeping, R. M. was seeking God wholeheartedly ... M. and S. were both crying at the altar ... It was beautiful to see God's presence ... I then introduced eighteen new members.[88]

The next eleven years brought ups and downs in the journey, as pastorates do. Throughout the years the church would average weekly approximately 350-400 people. On September 8, 2002, exactly ten years after becoming the pastor, we held the dedication service of a new sanctuary (Phase 2), inviting back the living former pastors, including the now re-married pastor I had followed. Contemporary worship Psalmist, Terry MacAlmon (at the time acclaimed for writing the worship chorus, "I Sing Praises to Your Name") came as special guest, and the keynote address was given by Ecuadorian missionary Bill McDonald (who would only a few years later found Unison International Television that would reach hundreds of thousands with the gospel message across Latin America).

My journal entry that day said, "Dedication Service, 571 in attendance. Grateful. Tired." Pastoral ministry is hard work. Think of it. It took nine years, in this case, from the one-year anniversary of completing Phase One, to seeing the construction of Phase Two and the growing of the church to this point, from the 300 range (a growth of 200+ in the first year, as I started with less than 100), to the 600 range (nearly doubling that over a period that took nine more long and laboring years). Some would say, "Well, that's not a huge church." Others will relate with me. It was exactly where I was to be, and became a miracle story within itself of a small church that found themselves seeing extraordinary things through God's favor. It was a type of what I've come to call, the Church of America; typically, smaller, often rural (our church was surrounded by horse farms), and with a precious touch of – family and God's presence.

My last service as the pastor of the church after having been elected district superintendent was twenty-one months later, June 6, 2004. It was the specific week of our sixteenth anniversary with the church. That day we rejoiced in what God had done in our twelve years as lead pastor, which included the 40 acres, nearly $5 million in assets and facilities, a full complement of paid staff, ministry from what had been developed as the largest daycare and pre-school in a tri-county area with twenty-five full-time employees and one hundred fifty children, individuals born again and water baptized at that juncture in almost every Sunday morning worship service weekly, and $430,000 that year in missions giving above tithes disbursed locally, across the United States, and internationally. All the years we pastored, I simply didn't want to be a church that solely dispensed goods and services. I wanted to make disciples who would make disciples, and do it on a global scale.

 I wanted to make disciples who would make disciples, and do it on a global scale.

That final service also highlighted another missionary window (our church was averaging hosting three missionaries per month at the time) and thirty-five new members joining the church. The invited guest missionary sat beside me that morning as the service began. He began to sense something unique about this particular service. I remember as if it were yesterday him leaning over and whispering in my ear the question, "Are you leaving today? Resigning?" I smiled with the response, "Why, yes. Did I not tell you? But, you have no worries. Missions is my heartbeat. Our people carry it as well. We are going to celebrate a glorious sixteen years and commit prayer and finances to your work." That day, I think several thousand dollars was given to his mission ministry, and he later thanked me again for caring so much for missions to have a guest missionary on the last day I was to serve the church.

All of these accomplishments are wonderful for a local church, pastor, and leaders. But, of most importance are the looming questions of "Did they see Jesus in me?" Through it all "...what was the overall impact of the role I played, or that of the church in revival for our city?"

It was a special season that occurred from 1995 through 1997 that is the focus here-forth. On Sunday, June 1, 1997, (nine years after arriving on staff at the church and almost five years after becoming the pastor) I wrote in my journal, "Each week the Lord moves differently, but each week He is faithful to minister to us. His glory falls week to week. For about two years now we've continued to witness special outpourings of His presence. They seem to come in seasons."[89] One such season lasted twelve weeks consecutively as altars were filled each service with dozens of people weeping and repenting, being saved, and being filled with the baptism of the Holy Spirit, often during the worship service and before, during and/or after the preaching of the Word.

Did revival end there? Was it deemed a three-month season out of a two-year snapshot of the entirety of the pastorate? No, revival did not end with this exclusive period of time. There were two most unique years. There were three months that absolutely changed my life. But, as was just described above, the story of this revival and in this ministry lasted the entire twelve years of our pastorate. It was nothing less than miraculous experiencing blessings of the sovereign hand of God. The overall ministry saw continued vivid encounters with God's presence, worship services that were so anointed with God's presence that one could seemingly touch it, and all witnessed in the lives of the people. It saw the exploding of global missions ministries locally and abroad, and numbers of individuals from those families and within the church who entered ministry from a laity or professional sense. At this writing, nearly twenty-five years later, I am reminded of how those years impacted so many. Revival changes everything.

Lessons: What Was Learned from This Revival Season?

For years, I have looked in the rearview mirror of life and ministry, endeavoring to interpret what occurred during these months of Holy Spirit visitation in our church and in my life. Analyzing what was learned from this Kentucky revival experience, I begin with the importance of speaking life, hope, and promises for God's Church. Pastors should learn the lifelong lesson of speaking hope and favor. Brownsville Revival pastor, John Kilpatrick said, "Pastors should speak fertility rather than sterility. Pray blessings over your church. When you are blessing the people and they are blessing you in prayer it's hard for the devil to get into that. Division disappears and unity appears."[90] Harmony is a necessity for the Pentecostal experience. When division occurs revival fires collapse.

Additionally learned was a lesson of love. During the height of outpouring in our church's altars and parishioner's homes, we were blessed that love and unity permeated our church as a standard characteristic, but not without challenges. The mark of the Holy Spirit is love. I continued to pray, "Open my eyes. Open the eyes of my heart, Lord." Love surprises and transcends individual understanding. The Holy Spirit brought heightened attention and focus to everything around me. It was as if my actual perception was more focused than any year previously. During this season strides were made simultaneously in areas of church growth, outreach, missions passion and giving, soul winning, and facilities development as evidenced in the ministry upon my leaving the pastorate some years later. Now, with nearly twenty years (at this writing) of denominational, pastoring pastors, and mentoring next-gen leaders, I wonder if pastors should focus less on the church-growth business and more on the changing-lives business. We need to lead the church as God intended it, not as we envision it.

Pastoring this revival, I learned that as quickly as revival comes, revival can depart. The spiritual warfare was intense and at times draining. Sometimes it was my own fault. Other times it was various situations or people within the ministries that stirred discontent. It brought new meaning (to me) of "...seek His presence continually..." (1 Chronicles 16:11, ESV). I found comfort in challenges by an overwhelming sense that I was genuinely hearing from and following the Lord, though I did not see clearly as to where it was going to lead. Philip Freeman wrote of St. Patrick of Ireland in the midst of his challenges, "What he did have going for him was a passionate conviction that he was right."[91] There were days during this season that it would seem ministry moments were being lived out on mountain top experiences only to have the appearance of falling crushingly to the ground the next day with conflicts and confusions. Learning to pastor a season of revival is a perplexing task. Loving people is not always as easy as it sounds. It requires intimacy with God and countless hours of bible study and prayer.

> *I learned that as quickly as revival comes, revival can depart. The spiritual warfare was intense and at times draining.*

Pastors carry duty and obligation in the calling of God. I further knew it was my own responsibility to welcome and willingly open myself to the Spirit's infilling and work. That's challenging to you and to others when you, yourself, ask God to come and do something supernatural in you. As Brian Edwards writes regarding God's divine presence, "Revival does not begin in a theology, but in a theophany. It begins in a revelation of Jesus Christ Himself and a sense of nearness of the Master."[92]

What Instigated the Revival Season?
The Word of God in Preaching and Worship

Worship services and the music of the church were directed to intense worship, songs *to* God more often than *about* Him, and great anthems of the Church, both from modern choruses and traditional hymns. I preached doctrinal messages. I preached sermons on revival and hungering for God. I preached repentance. People on earth hate to hear the word repent. I heard it preached once, "Those in hell wish they could hear it just once more." I preached holiness. I preached reverence. I preached missionally. It was my job to be faithful and preach the Word as the Lord directed my heart, trusting God himself to do His work through it.

Iain H. Murray says of revival, "I do not believe the preacher can make the word preached by him effectual to the conversion of sinners. If they faithfully preached, that was their duty. What effect it should produce was the divine prerogative to determine."[93] Sermons about preparing the altar and tabernacle of our lives for God's presence to visit us, being set apart, teachings on prayer, anointing, even anointing oil and prayer cloths, were common themes. "Revival preaching has a power and authority that bring the Word of God like a hammer to the heart and conscience."[94] God's word cannot simply or solely be lived before a pastor's flock. It must be faithfully applied, and scripturally expounded upon daily.

Altar Calls, the Laying on of Hands, and Prayer

One of my 1997 journal entries read,

> I prayed with one lady and I literally felt the power of God run through me and it hit her like a lightning bolt. She fell... sometimes when I pray over others I won't even touch them. I'll start to pray over them and just lift my hand and they'll fall; slain in the Spirit. God's power is incomprehensible... I'm needing God to begin to speak to me about the revival services... I need you, God.[95]

Revival at King's Way Assembly Versailles, KY (1997)

This was a season where nothing seemed to make sense to the pastor. Most things occurring, I was not sure even I understood. However, I knew that I sensed—as did others—a hovering of the Holy Spirit in our services that could not be explained. It was the most unique presence of God I had ever experienced. The diversity of congregants, some lifelong Pentecostals, others years-faithful Baptists, Methodists, and Catholics, Lutherans, Episcopalians, and more all seemed to acknowledge this unique season of inexpressible glory. In one service an Episcopal priest who often worshipped with us on Sunday evenings testified to me of receiving the Baptism in the Holy Spirit while standing during worship in one of our services! I was intent upon listening to God's still small voice and discernment. I would often in a service, simply stand in silence at the pulpit in God's presence, purposefully giving those moments of holy reverence to the Lord, Himself, as a gift. He never disappointed. His manifest presence was evident.

It became paramount to implement a prayer ministry. Sure, we all have prayer in church, right? But, do we? During this season I added a part-time staff person, a seasoned man of prayer and the Word who had been a minister on a number of church staff's previously before his retirement, to lead our prayer ministries. At one time, over twenty-five percent of our church was praying and fasting weekly with special prayer teams praying on a scheduled basis during our Sunday morning services. Now more than ever the Church's leaders must create environments where Spirit-empowered prayer is not a program or ministry, but it is the main focus for everything else that happens in our work for the Lord. Some people are natural worriers. Others are natural warriors. I found warriors who made the difference in every arena. I found people hungering to be transformed and who trusted in what they sensed God was saying even when they didn't understand or see what He was doing. When it seemed

> *Some people are natural worriers. Others are natural warriors. I found warriors who made the difference in every arena.*

time to vent, they instead prayed. Revival is about returning to the Lord, returning to one's first love, returning for deeper waters, a pressing in, and an expecting for more of God's fullness.

"Then you will call on me and come and pray to me, and I will listen to you. You will seek me and find me when you seek me with all your heart" (Jeremiah 29:12-13, NIV).

A Commitment to Missions and Soul Winning

Missions and soul winning became my burden with a growing vision to disciple other pastors and churches in doing the same by ourselves become a leading missions church in the state and in my church's fellowship, the Assemblies of God. It has been said that a church will start to die when it works to keep people rather than reach people. Multiple missionary services were added to our schedules, allowing each a fifteen-minute window to share their heart and burden. As pastor, I would receive an offering for each person, believing that a prepared honorarium given to a missionary would undermine the work of the Holy Spirit. As pastor, it was important to me to give God the opportunity to do what He so desired in the hearts of people, rather than me making the decision for Him by giving a missionary worker a pre-arranged offering. And, week after week following the church's already received tithes and offerings, extra missionary offerings would see thousands of dollars given joyously. People give to what they believe in.

Multiple missions trips for our congregants were scheduled annually with dozens of our members joining the teams regularly. Within ten years, the church increased missions giving from approximately $10,000 to $430,000 annually in the denomination's Kentucky District through both foreign and local mission initiatives. A deepening commitment to preaching and training our congregants to share their faith personally in their daily lives began seeing newcomers joining for attendance, getting baptized, and sharing their testimonies to the church. Discipleship took on a new meaning for the shaping of our ministry initiatives. The last few years of our pastorate, we held baptisms during every Sunday morning worship service.

Preparation and Expectancy

Often, many people responded at altars—some with silent tears streaming down their faces and others with open weeping. Others would sit in their pews/chairs with peace upon their faces. When you see that depth of seeking the Lord, the church is on the precipice of things only the Lord can comprehend. I was grateful to see hungering hearts. As Leonard Ravenhill wrote of the American Church, "...our eyes are dry...God pity us!"[96] It appeared as if the entirety of our church began expecting something from God at each gathering. For the first time, I was beginning to understand the concept of expectation. There was suspense, even anticipation.

Not understanding exactly what God wanted to do from service to service, as mentioned, I found myself often standing quiet and still before the Lord and the people at the pulpit, having walked carefully to center stage following a time of intimate worship. I pray God will teach me to listen beyond words. It was not uncommon that I would stand in this awe of silence for two, three, what seemed five minutes without one word uttered as the congregation and I stood in a tangible and manifest presence of God's holiness. As intercessor, Rees Howells, writes, "It took a little time before I could learn to be absolutely quiet in His presence."[97] I had learned to be content with such silence.

> *It appeared as if the entirety of our church began expecting something from God at each gathering.*

Hunger was growing in the hearts of the people, and they began seeking the Lord with fervency. Edward Miller wrote of the Argentine revival when people began seeking the Lord, "the Holy Spirit began to visit them."[98] With inexplicable outpourings of the Holy Spirit at regular morning church services, I was encouraged to attend a pastor's conference at Northwest Assembly of God in Dublin, Ohio, being conducted by Brownsville Revival Pastor John Kilpatrick. On July 30, 1996, my journal entry reads, "...the things I'm experiencing right now are unlike anything I've ever experienced before ... I don't understand all of this—don't pretend to. But ... I know ... it's God."[99] It was written of Cane Ridge revivalist, James McGready, who "when he came to examine his feelings ... it seemed to him that he did not understand these things."[100] I felt much the same.

What Brought Decline to the Revival Season? (A Personal Assessment)

Many years have passed since this particular revival outpouring at that local church in Kentucky. Never to place blame on others, I have come to the conclusion the decline in the revival was much attributed to my own lack of pastoral leadership. Was I unfaithful? No. Did I fall away in temptations? No. Did I purposefully affront people or do any number of misdeeds? No. Did I continue to faithfully pray? Yes. Did I faithfully preach the Word? Yes. Did I lead the church in moving toward the deeper things of God? Yes. Was I faithful to my wife and my children? Yes. Then, how could it be my fault? I'm not saying that it was. But, I own the fact that much of the responsibility of stewarding a revival lays at the discerning and apostolic leadership of the pastor.

Much of the responsibility of stewarding a revival lays at the discerning and apostolic leadership of the pastor.

Though the challenge of acceptance in today's Church has continued, it appears that conventional, contemporary Christian denominations have offered little to the discussion or general recognition of the apostolic calling or function in today's church, whereas charismatic fellowships generally are more accepting. While spiritual roles of pastors, teachers, and evangelists have readily been accepted by mainstream Christian cultures, the seasoned mantles of prophetic and apostolic gifts are likewise essential for a balanced maturity as coheirs and partakers in the kingdom of God (See: Ephesians 4:11; 1 Corinthians 12-14).

A season of revival must always have the shepherd's leadership. The pastor can neither delegate it to another nor let it glide, assuming that the rich worship environment is sufficient to keep it moving in the right direction without question. If it drifts rampantly without balance, then the enemy will have his way in the lives of faithful seekers. A revival must be stewarded. Discernment is imperative. Souls must continue as the emphasis. The fruit of this holy season is seen in lives changed and cities transformed.

During the confusing days of unexplained manifestations, I found my heart open and hungry for more of God, trusting and pure in motive, but untrained and inexperienced to lead revival. Unfortunately, I further suffered by having few close friends to lean on, inquire of, or sit down with to process and pray through all that was occurring. Certainly there were people I could have called. I should have called them. But, I didn't. Too many of our leaders today are in the same situation if they are honest with themselves. We cannot be isolated. We must allow God-directed relationships to assist us with wisdom and discernment.

My assessment is that it began to unravel as congregants, given influence as spiritual leaders, were granted freedom by the pastor (me) to lead and flow freely in five-fold ministry gifts (Ephesians 4). Freedom is not the right to do as one pleases but the opportunity to do what is right. There is no cessation of a need for Spirit-empowered leaders to be committed to holiness, understand the need for planting, developing, training, and mentoring others in the church or maintaining a willingness and authority to rebuke and discipline those harming the people of God and distorting God's truth. Pentecostal leaders must be accountable, remain discerning, prayerfully prepared to lead, and Spirit-directed in all they do. Imbalanced, abusive, and false apostolic approaches, while sounding and appearing authoritative, eloquent, or spiritually defining to a searching audience, will always lack in one or more of these values. Today's church and her leaders must be on guard for unhealthy apostolic imposters and self-imposed apostolic or prophetic leaders who will guide unsuspecting and well-meaning seekers of truth astray. Further, it appears multitudes within the church and Para-church cultures flock to prophetic conferences across the globe but are not found at their local pastor's bible study or prayer group. Today's church needs an awakening. You can't pour from an empty cup. Take care of yourself. Grow in the Lord.

It's essential.

"For I will pour water on the thirsty land, and streams on the dry ground; I will pour out My Spirit on your offspring, and My blessing on your descendent" (Isaiah 44:3, NIV).

The prophetic gifts became more prominent than had previously been offered in our church. Individual personalities became evident and involved in the way ministry was being offered to attendees. For example, some individuals would be loud at times, as if they were yelling at the devil as they prayed over individuals. Other leaders were too forceful with the laying on of hands. Some leaders would seem to be pushing people over when they would pray for them at altars. At one service, I as pastor had relinquished the microphone to a perceived spiritual leader who had come to me and asked if he could share with the people. By the end of that evening, there were many who had seemingly been slain in the Spirit, but confusion was apparent.

I distinctly remember asking myself silently, of course, thinking it to myself, "What is happening here? I do not understand this, Lord. Is this of You?" Whether pastors are deeply mature in the Lord or new to the calling of God and inexperienced, God himself grants His gift and calling to them. When pastors question in confusion experiences within services, the revival has drifted, and trouble mounts.

The Monday following this service, a member of the church who had been prayed for by one of our congregants who had pushed him at the altar called my office explaining he had received a broken rib when he received prayer and had fallen at the church. Remorseful, I immediately apologized to the Lord and to the man on the phone, explaining to him that if he received a broken rib, it was not of the Lord and I, as pastor, had not protected him. I asked his forgiveness immediately. To my dismay, he responded with a rebuke to me, saying, that my apology to him proved his discernment was correct in that I was "not a man of faith and power, but rather a skeptic," assuring me it had been "fully of God" and was his own fault because of the way he had fallen. Again, I was numb and confused, startled and overwhelmed at the response and disrespect received. The gentleman on the phone continued that he would be leaving the church, not because of his rib being broken or the church service in question, but because he could no longer stay at a church or under the covering of a pastor who he believed lacked faith.

It appeared at this season of the ministry that there were challenges at every turn. I felt as though I had fallen and could never stand again. Unity was faltering, and because of that, coordinated prayer, weakened. Winkie Pratney writes that "The two essential conditions of revival are unity and prayer."[101] It was during this season that I learned this—the one who falls and gets up is so much stronger than the one who never falls. That statement was directed to me, not the one who had called me regarding his literal fall. I was the one that needed to stand up—and stand up stronger. When you kneel before God, He stands up for you. And when God stands up for you, no one can stand against you.

It's never been a challenge to encounter struggles. Too often we're blind to God's amazing work and plan. If anything I've learned in my quest for the Lord's presence it is that He is faithful. All my life He has been faithful. His grace, His mercy, and His kindness is ever at my door awaiting my heart and hand to receive of Him. His provision and His presence is promised.

What Challenges Were Observed, and How Were They Handled during This Revival Season?

Integrity, Character, and Witness

Numerous issues of integrity and character emerged during the season of revival. The call of perfecting the saints and trainging ministers to be sent for a global mandate and harvest begins with the character of those sending. Deep unity that had existed so beautifully among leaders, staff, and parishioners became challenged. As pastor, I found myself dealing with issues our church had previously avoided. Lack of reverence and respect, modesty challenges in dress from among attendees and members, waning church attendance, weakened service, and financial giving were all declining. Further, involvement from key leadership, lawsuits, materialism, sexual purity matters, gossip, pride, matters of truth, integrity and more challenged my experience and wisdom at every turn. I would go home at times so discouraged that I wondered if I could survive yet another month. I knew from deep within my soul that whatever was bringing me down was already beneath me, yet I felt the weight of it all.

> *I would go home at times so discouraged that I wondered if I could survive yet another month.*

Further, personality issues with certain key church influencers and with central music and worship team participants brought turmoil and burden weekly. I was hurting. They were hurting. Long-time members randomly left the church.

Claudio Freidzon (pastor of the church Rey de Reyes, a congregation of over 20,000 members in Belgrano, Buenos Aires) writes, "The dove of the Holy Spirit rests on men and women who are meek and forgiving. Bitterness, accusations, resentment, and criticism grieve the Spirit."[102] Freidzon writes of

> three requirements for achieving the anointing of God upon our lives: being united in love (Ephesians 4:1-3), exercising the pertinent gift that one has received (Romans 12:3-4), and obeying those who are in authority over us while accepting and receiving counsel from the brethren (Romans 13:1, Ephesians 5:21).[103]

Yet, I found it oddly that altars continued to fill with hearts yearning for more, and lives were being radically changed in our midst. And, it was as if some of the strangest people of that geographical region's Charismatic and various Pentecostal circles began arriving for our services unsolicited. Where were they coming from?

How Were Challenges Handled?

A myriad of approaches were necessary to deal with the destructive behaviors evidenced in the church. One-on-one meetings with antagonists were conducted. The face-to-face sit down meetings are paramount for addressing such concerns. Those cannot be delegated. Pastors must have such meetings personally. Policies of confidentiality and documentation were followed as closely as possible. Public comments were made sparingly but were offered when they would bring pastoral strength to the ministry. Denominational support was sought from our district's executive pastors. They were mature men of prayer with years of pastoral leadership and experience. More than one special-called board meeting lasted past midnight as leaders of the church discussed the growing pains and challenges faced week to week. As pastor, I implemented annual pastor-board-staff retreats for relationship building and extended times of prayer together. Prayer teams were strengthened and further developed.

Visionary, pace-setting, and strategic leadership became problematic, as I was addressing challenging issues repeatedly. At one intense meeting with the church worship team related to conflict within, tears flowed, humility was offered, some expressed frustrations and anger, but the shocking pastoral decision to remove the entire worship team for an extended period to be determined in progress remained. They looked at me in awe. What would we do? Are you crazy? For the interim, I found a new team to lead beginning the next Sunday morning.

That decision changed the course of our worship for years to come. The worship team of gifted singers and musicians was welcomed back to the platform to again lead worship for our services one year later. All of them stayed with the church during that time except for one family. It was a miracle of healing that took place to see them return to ministry after having been asked to sit down from ministry for one year. To this day, the very ones who sat out of

> *Before you stand firm, make sure your feet are in the right place.*

their God-directed ministries for a year in confusion and despair became close and personal friends of integrity and respect. Now, twenty-five years later, the same church has yet an amazing worship ministry of anointed singers and musicians leading congregants weekly into the presence of God.

Lessons were learned. I'm still reminded that for those who choose such strong decisions, before you stand firm, make sure your feet are in the right place. I look back on those days, oft perplexed as I was, to see how God sovereignly protected and directed the church and her ministries bringing about an enormous miracle over the next few years to come.

Conclusion

As Carolyn Tennant notes, "A hallmark of great moves of God down through history is that they have been characterized by repentance, confession, contrition, and brokenness."[104] Without question, the revival experience and flowing current of the Holy Spirit written of in this chapter was evidenced by each of those attributes during the ebb and flow of this manifest move of God. True Christian leaders should be calling people to something greater than themselves and moving them to a place of expecting the unexpected.[105] There is no statute of limitations on the Spirit of God as to whom He calls or to what generation He calls one to. As Ruth Haley Barton writes, "Many of us have no idea how starving we are and that we are so far into the later stages of spiritual starvation that we don't know what it is to be full and well."[106] I desire to walk and live in His presence daily while surrounded by supernatural and transcendent intimacy with the triune Godhead.

Few Christians understand that realm. Fewer *want* to understand. My hunger remains to individually find and dwell within the constant spring of living water for revival flames in my life and within my family. Lessons learned from these experiences will resonate with me for all my remaining days on earth. The walk with God is a journey. If anything, I have learned to quit worrying about the potholes in the road and enjoy the journey ahead. I strive for personal revival and to be found faithful. It is my story.

Chapter 5

Leading for Revival

"Call to me and I will answer you, and will tell you great and hidden things that you have not known"
(Jeremiah 33:3, ESV).

NBA great, Michael Jordan, was said to have missed over 9000 shots in his career, lost nearly 300 games, and nearly 30 times was given the ball to hit the game-winning shot, yet failed in doing so. He attributed those lessons learned to why he became a success.

Not long ago, I sat across the dinner table from a credentialed minister sharing with me of the revival service and revivalist who'd preached years earlier when they had encountered the Lord in a powerful way. As a denominational superintendent I listened as that minister was not only recounting his testimony of the past revival, but now—those many years later—processing a moral failure that had ended years of faithful ministry and service.

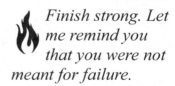
Finish strong. Let me remind you that you were not meant for failure.

Hold the line, friends. Finish strong. Let me remind you that you were not meant for failure. When you stumble. Go repentantly to the Lord. Get up. Get help, and finish the race. Jesus is for you. He's on your side. He's there for you. He's forever cheering you on.

Whether one considers St. Patrick's evangelistic transformation of Ireland, the Moravian Revival of Count Zinzendorf, David Brainard, the Wesley brothers, George Whitefield, Barton Stone, Jeremiah Lanphier, Dwight Moody, Aimee Simple McPherson, Kathryn Kuhlman, Oral Roberts, Billy Graham, or dozens of other names that one could add to the list, I think every revival leader wants to cross the finish line a winner. High school track coaches are notorious for telling their runners that the last third of a race was the most critical. Whether running sprints, middle distance, long distance, hurdles, or relays, the push to the finish line matters. We're all in a race of life. It would do us good to remind ourselves of the fundamentals. There aren't many gold medals passed out for the "85 yard" dash. Don't let life trip you up. Stay focused. Go the distance. Finish strong.

> *Don't let life trip you up. Stay focused. Go the distance. Finish strong.*

A friend and colleague of mine, Rev. Kristy Long, recently reminded me that she was not interested in ministry for the sake of ministry. She said she were not interested in ministry as the pursuit of a purpose. This credentialed woman of God, former (faithful and well-respected) pastor of a church, and dedicated wife and mother wrote that despite her flesh, her purpose for ministry did not rely within ministry. She had been created with a purpose and ministry flowed from her very being. She said, "Pursuit of platforms and pulpits disrupt peace and doubt purpose." There is such truth in that word. After she had left her pastorate she was once asked innocently (we assume) about what particular ministry position she held. She dropped her head in the moment aching shamefully as she responded she was no longer in ministry. A tear escaped her eye. Then, the Holy Spirit spoke to her spirit. Insignificant, unimportant, failure, and embarrassing were the condemning voices that filled her mind. Until, she heard His. She realized her life was ministry. If she never held another microphone, if she never stepped upon another platform, if she never beheld another pulpit, she would never forget that her life, everyday, ordinary, mundane, simple

Leading for Revival

as it seemed, was beautiful and fruitful ministry for her King. A presidential candidate once told an audience of ministers that he felt they'd lost their voice and he was going to help them get it back. I encourage if you've lost your voice, let the Holy Spirit help you get it back.

Another friend, Dr. Beth Grant said, (in so many words), "There are many voices. What matters is that you listen for His." Have you ever noticed as you go about your day the moments when you sense God leading you to do something particular, say something to the person at the counter, or go out of your way to accomplish something for someone else that He's laid upon your heart? Maybe you're walking the halls of a school, or standing in front of a class or group of colleagues, or driving down the road in your vehicle, or simply sitting quietly in an airport amidst the hustle and bustle of the crowds. There's an aspect of hearing from God that is dispositional. How you take in what someone else is communicating has to do with your disposition (character, temperament, mood, personality, outlook). Whether it is your children, grandchildren, contemporaries, teammates, church members, or others, their hearing you or what you've communicated just might have to do with what other sounds have drawn their attention. I travel weekly (for years) city to city, pulpit to pulpit, nation to nation. I am confident there is a generation arising that is absorbing and acquiring a keen ability to give God their undivided attention. They are highly attuned to the voice of God. What's your disposition? What voices are you hearing?

On a number of occasions, I have been asked to address Christian leadership principles. Speaking to an audience of about fifty people in Bulgaria years ago, an individual came to me following one of the sessions. Through the interpreter he shared how he had been so moved thinking about his own life and leadership as I offered, point-by-point, precepts that could have saved him many headaches. The lectures were a commitment to a long-term race. Leadership, missions, and ministry is not a sprint. It's a marathon journey.

In a recent guest lecture for a seminary doctoral class, I was asked my candid responses to six primary leadership questions. Similar questions had been on my radar and talk topics for years. To add some zest this time, I queried about a dozen colleagues from across the United States to see how their responses might coincide with my own. I was amazed to see the similarities. What I found in that exercise was a raw and straightforward précis of principal Christian ideologies that would set a course for health and distinction in leadership. As I shared in the previous chapter, finding trusted colleagues and friends who can share your insights and process with you your questions will bring you closer to the heart of God and His revival focus for your life and ministry leadership. Trusted voices from Jesus-faithful friends help you set the pace for longevity in leadership, ministry, and sound doctrine.

I have been blessed for decades with trustworthy, proficient, imaginative, resourceful, disciplined, and for the most part long-term leaders who have served alongside Renee and I throughout our years of ministry. From the local church, to Para church ministries, to denominational leadership, God has faithfully encouraged me with team members who have made me better in every sense.

In another of my books, *Setting the Atmosphere for the Day of Worship – II*, I offered a specified chapter on the variations between bosses, managers, or supervisors and indisputably authentic leaders. Such authentic leaders function from generosity, care, and liberality. They educate, impart, and communicate. They inspire, reassure, and produce enthusiasm, relevance, and expectancy. They are proactive and steadfast. Such leaders convey peace and challenge for distinction, quality, and merit. Each of these gifts are paramount for a pastor-leader leading revival.

"You can sleep peacefully. God is awake."

I remind leaders, "You can sleep peacefully. God is awake." Leaders participate with the group and show the way, fostering

Leading for Revival

development. And, like the 1990s purple dinosaur character, Barney advocated, leaders still say, "Please" and "Thank You." If you're not doing those things, you're simply a boss and unquestionably not equipped with primary Christian leadership values, ethics, and ideologies.

I've met and known, as have you, a number of gifted and talented leaders through the years. They have had notable abilities and strengths. One such leader in my story is as accomplished a musician, as any pastor would desire to lead worship in his or her church. I've often thought, to this day, how I don't understand. The moment this person's fingers touched a piano keyboard, the anointing seemed rich and drawing. And yet, the individual has lived certain matters of their personal life questionable to many. We speak of spiritual gifts. It's leadership. I am reminded of Romans 11:29 that tells us the gifts of God are fixed, binding, and irreversible. None have received leadership or gifts because we merit them. But shouldn't the anointing leave a person whose lifestyles and leadership are questionable? No. Anointing denotes sanctification – being set apart. God has granted and allowed anointing for the advantage and profit of those who would receive of Him. He doesn't grant anointing to benefit the one with the gift(s). It's all about Jesus.

Sin will mark you blind to your own culpabilities. Sin is an expensive venture. You'll find yourself paying far more than you had anticipated. A sea of suffering is better than a solitary dewdrop of sin. I find leaders of all kinds deal with the unforeseen waylay—an enemy's ambush that thwarts the roadmap of leadership. Whether it's money, extramarital affairs, fame, pride, sexual perversion, an unheeded family, or a myriad of other scenarios to end what God intended as good, the leader must stay aligned to God himself. It isn't always what it seems. Sometimes poor leadership is found in what the world would say is most honorable. The church has a number of workaholics.

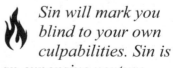

Sin will mark you blind to your own culpabilities. Sin is an expensive venture.

75

I remind parents reading this that the most important hours of your week are the ones you spend at home. When my life's days are nearing their end, it will be as nothing and meaningless if I haven't transferred my faith in Christ to my children. I smiled this past week when I received a photo of my two-year-old grandson on a mid-day outing with his dad. My son, living and working in New York City, had found a rare moment when his hospital schedule changed and opted to take advantage of the moment to pick up little James from his daily routine of nursery/pre-school. They spent the day – a great surprise for James – together with fun, love, and laughter. Remind your children, of all the kids in the world, you'd choose them. The church instills faith. You are the church. Rapidly changing culture will see our structures, buildings and a weekend event or service as less impactful to changed lives. Shifting global cultures are affecting today's Church and challenging her standards for doctrinal purity. Disciples making disciples will continue. Faith will grow. Miracles will continue. The church will thrive.

Give your children the ability to see themselves as you do. They will recognize how special they are – to you. Pray for them. Pray with them. And, remind them often that your prayers for them are daily and consistent. One of the best parenting quotes I've ever heard (author unknown) was, "As a parent, it's my priority to help you get into Heaven, not Harvard." I'm not saying Harvard would be so bad. I'm clearly saying keep the fire burning on the altar. Do not let it burn out. Hold the line, friends. Finish strong.

More than once, I've heard the response, "I was doing okay, until…" Until, what? Something happened. I went to… I asked if I could… I thought just this once wouldn't hurt. I thought no one would know. I went the wrong way. Sin is subtle. Sometimes it can seem as though you're paddling in a river upstream. I've sat with a number of men and women who have admitted adultery or any number of other sordid and painful sins, moral and ethical. Every sexual failure is first met by emotional calamity. Every sinful act, moment, mistake, and disappointment is from a drifting contempt and neglect of God. Someone once said, "A mistake that makes you humble is better than an achievement that makes you arrogant." If only the church's leaders would read God's Word.

> "But after Uzziah became powerful, his pride led to his downfall. He was unfaithful to the LORD his God..." (2 Chron. 26:16, NIV).

Staying in God's Word grounds the leader, providing more than personal stability, and builds a Spirit-useful foundation for effective ministry. The person of the Holy Spirit invests in leaders by using God's Word in them to do supernatural works for the kingdom. Our devotion to and received callings of God as leaders of His Church takes us willingly off the shore and into territories that can only be overcome by a Spirit-filled work and workers. Faithful service for apostolic leaders has not abated. Answering the call of God is the initial step for such a kingdom worker. The apostolic is a mandatory functioning if the Church is to move forward.

The Church needs an encounter with God and leaders with apostolic initiative to pursue it.

A pastor shepherds the flock or the church. An evangelist is committed to outreach and proclaiming of good news to those outside the Church. A prophet calls out sin, interprets the will of God, and/or foretells through the Spirit's unction that which is to come. But an apostle, while he or she may do each of the above, primarily casts vision and carries a critical role of a spiritual pioneer in our shifting, multi-cultural world – developing, initiating, establishing, discovering, forging, inventing, and innovating new paths for the faith. Undeniably, the Church still needs leaders today who will invade the darkness and take the gospel where it has never been before. Such leadership is that of both strength and humility, dedicated to the calling rather than title or position. This mantle of leadership provides both boundaries and purpose as the Holy Spirit gives the increase and directives. The gospel is offensive calling all who receive it to a reformed and improved life. The Church needs an encounter with God and leaders with apostolic initiative to pursue it.

Revival leaders must be renewed. Those leaders who are spiritually renewed and recharged will lead others into and through revival. Such leaders will lead the way. I wrote in Redemptive Missiology in Pneumatic Context that grace is for the lowly, not the lofty. And, for the believer, it is good to remember that God cannot help the Christian who is proud. I am convinced God is raising up a generation of revival-hungry and Jesus-faithful leaders who will not follow the norms or walk with the crowds. Their posture will be a standard above, living by a challenged call. The church needs men and women with an Isaiah call. In Isaiah 6:1–13, he cried, "I am undone."

> *We've a need for an anointed group of Pentecostal leaders in today's world. Find out what God is doing and what God is blessing.*

- Be a voice as one crying in the wilderness, to today's Church, as lukewarm-ness and complacency overtake God's people.
- Ask God to break you—that you might be useful to Him and His work.
- Walk in humility, regardless of where God takes you.
- Hunger for God's presence. Redemption power comes from the secret place of the Holy Spirit.
- Ask God for discernment as you look for the needy and their needs so that redemption might flow through you.

We've a need for an anointed group of Pentecostal leaders in today's world. Find out what God is doing and what God is blessing. Therein spend your time, build your church, and expend all your efforts and resources.

- Where do I see God at work?
- Where and how is God working in the lives of those around me?
- Where and how is God working in my neighborhood?
- In light of my gifts and resources, how does God want me to partner with Him in what He is doing?

There is no other reason for a church's existence, but that we would reach the lost—at all cost. The closer God's people get to Him the more they realize how beneath their inheritance they have lived. I pray the nations will be granted godly leaders who will lead for revival, the revived church, and the awakening of blinded eyes to the hope and promises of Jesus Christ.

> *There is no other reason for a church's existence, but that we would reach the lost—at all cost.*

Chapter 6

Suffering, Serving, and Seeking throughout a Pandemic

"Comfort, comfort my people, says your God. Speak tenderly to Jerusalem, and cry to her that her warfare is ended, that her iniquity is pardoned, that she has received from the Lord's hand double for all her sins. A voice cries: "In the wilderness prepare the way of the Lord; make straight in the desert a highway for our God. Every valley shall be lifted up, and every mountain and hill be made low; the uneven ground shall become level, and the rough places a plain. And the glory of the Lord shall be revealed, and all flesh shall see it together, for the mouth of the Lord has spoken"
(Isaiah 40:1-10, ESV)

COVID-19 and the World

In early 2020 the pandemic of COVID-19 brought devastating effects internationally that lasted well into 2021, with impacts for years to come, before an initial vaccine began to stem the tide of this terrible disease. Little did one know at the time that new strains of the virus would soon arise and fears would grip nations again. A Yale Medicine review reported the Delta variant was described as more contagious than the common cold and influenza, or the viruses triggering Ebola, smallpox, MERS, and SARS. The peak spread of cases fall within low immunization environments, and nearly all serious circumstances and deaths have been among the unvaccinated, according to the (Centers for Disease Control) CDC. The Church is challenged with maintaining unity and harmony amidst a divisive political agenda, which emerged from pandemic topics and subject matter. In August 2021, I sat in an Orlando hotel listening to news reports that the state of Florida had reported 21,683 new cases of COVID-19 in one day of that week, the state's highest one-day total since the start of the pandemic (data from the Centers for Disease Control and Prevention). The new strain being called "Delta variant" was again sweeping the nation(s). Times of crisis lead the courageous – the devoted - to prayer. Prayer leads the Church to revival.

Those living in the 2020's are not the first to endure hardship. My grandfathers both served in World War I. In 1914 the war began leaving 22 million people dead. Thereafter, "Spanish Flu" killed 50 million people. By the end of another decade the New York Stock Exchange collapsed leading to a global economic crisis. Within five more years the Nazis came to power and by the end of that decade World War II encountered the Holocaust and six million Jews were martyred. Yad Vashem, Israel's principal Holocaust memorial, sits at the Mount of Remembrance on the outskirts of Jerusalem. I've been there. It's sobering.

My father was a college student at a small Kentucky college when the unthinkable occurred. From the bombing of Pearl Harbor (December 7, 1941) and what soon then occurred in Japan will long be remembered as a decisive moment in the prevailing chronicle of America and the world. My dad immediately enlisted in the US Army and was soon sent to ... Pearl Harbor, Hawaii. America's response to the Pearl Harbor incident determined the outcome of the Second World War. More than that, it fashioned the providence of a dream that liberty and independence could withstand in this world. Albeit, pain and suffering to be caused and inflicted was inconceivable. Overall some 75 million individuals died in World War II, including approximately 20 million military personnel and 40 million civilians, many of who died because of meditative massacre, mass-bombings, related sicknesses, illnesses, diseases, and famine.

While this modern-day 21st century suffering, pandemic, four-and-a-half million deaths (to date) globally, and crushing international economic downturns altered the state of the church for a myriad of reasons, revival became a topic across the world once again. Suffering, serving, and seeking might well relate to finding that secret place relationship (revival) with the Master. Amidst it all, I see hunger for the things of God and a great desire for an encounter with Him.

As countries shut down, economies collapsed, and hospitals were overrun. Some nations had thousands of people dying daily in their homes, hospitals, care facilities, and even in the streets. In one day, New York City had more deaths to COVID-19 than any other nation in the world. We were witnessing before our eyes how a worldwide pandemic could readily bring global economic structures to halt and thrust societies into new ways of doing business never before imagined.

This pandemic challenged conversations as discussions regarding social distancing, catching something, or spreading one's own viruses to another dominated news stories and personal dialogues alike. Not since the 1918 Flu had nations shut down economies, churches, and family routines in this nature. Groceries, warehouses, and retailers of numerous kinds implemented varying degrees of protocols. Stores limited the numbers of items you could purchase, and most roped off areas or taped floors with the "X" to tell people where to stand 6' apart or away from employees. Globally men and women were required to wear facemasks and coverings. High school and university graduations and celebrations became virtual or reduced to a drive-by ten-minute event.

This time of the pandemic was also a politically charged time in our nation. The old normal was to never return. A new normal was emerging. At one moment during the turmoil, our state's newly-elected Attorney General prepared to sue our newly-elected Governor, and just as citizens of the Great

Depression carried the scars of that event for decades to come, the halted economy, the pain of nearly 40 percent of Kentuckians (the state where I reside) who were forced to file for unemployment within the first three months of the 2020 pandemic, and worship facilities having been closed with religious liberties challenged, left deep wounds—personal, psychological, and spiritual—for some, unbearable and unforgettable.

A new normal was emerging.

The nations realized their vulnerability. Unexpected and overwhelming death dominated the news. Yet, in the midst of it all, a groundswell of gratitude overcame the nations. My own New York City physician son and daughter-in-law stood at 17th-floor windows overlooking their Manhattan apartment skyline and the streets below for months listening to the weekly applause from those lining city streets, balconies, and open windows of high-rises as citizens applauded health-care workers and first responders for front-line efforts in fighting the virus. My physician wife and her colleagues joined the ranks of those serving on the front-line of this new battle and developed further the efforts for tele-medicine. Ministry leader colleagues around the nation contended with how to conduct large-attendance events via digital means and electronic voting. Modern enterprise video communication and audio-conferencing companies changed the way our grass roots businesses across the nation conducted business. Suddenly, though distanced from loved-ones in other locals, immediate families were eating meals at home again together.

Governments, attempting to stem the tide, implemented social restrictions that challenged religious freedoms, and some faith-based institutions resisted such efforts. This was a time of great challenge and yet opportunity for Christians, the Church, and its Leaders.

COVID-19, the Church, and Its Leaders

God is good even when life isn't. When life isn't good and we are so shaken, such experiences reveal our flaws and weaknesses. It's been said for years that crisis reveals character. How one reacts speaks volumes. Don't be reactionary. I've told people for years they didn't need to respond to every comment, post, or action of another. Sometimes (most times) a simple refrain allows the Holy Spirit to do His work. Too often, troubling responses from the Church during this crisis sent bizarre and disconcerting perceptions to the greater segments of society. While that was unfortunate, most Christians tried their best to live deeply prayerful lives with high expectations that God was still at work in the world through this watershed of death and confusion, disruption and economic downfall.

> *God is good even when life isn't.*
> *When life isn't good and we are so shaken, such experiences reveal our flaws and weaknesses.*

Early in the months of home isolation, I penned these words:

Alien Days ©

Warriors stand restless for liberties mistreated. Nations lay idle and markets depleted. Questions linger in uncertain times. Hospitals fill with sobering chimes. The Church holds firm with truth completed. The world concerned; unseated; retreated. Hope most divine in mysterious prime. Good redefined inexplicable sublime. No other name but He above all. Author of joy for those who call.

Joseph S. Girdler, DMin / 4.20.2020

Pastors wrestled with voices from multiple directions. Many said they couldn't open worship centers because of health risks and that they'd be wrong to do so. Others roared "hoax" and said the restrictions were just the result of media frenzy. Culture found a new level of suspicion for science. Cynicism was rampant. Slanted rationality, vicars of conspiracy philosophies, phony news, and party-political grandiloquence were rampant. Alarm of microchips, government conspiracy, and "Big pharma" filled social media. Simultaneously, news reports spread of spouses, parents, grandparents, and children passing away from COVID-19.

Government regulations and step-by-step procedures to prepare ministries for re-opening became problematic for several. Weekly, I would encourage the hundreds of ministers in our fellowship with words such as these:

> I am beyond proud of you regarding your leadership during this unique hour in our nation's history. God is using you. Lead with hope. Lead with faith. Lead with wisdom. We will continue to communicate as often and as efficiently as possible.

That communication systematically took on a life of its own in the weeks to ensue. I challenged myself to lead in new ways. The Superintendent's Tuesday-Text, Wednesday-Written Update document, and the Thursday Superintendent's Zoom became regular weekly parts of leadership. A leader-shift takes place when a man or woman is selected to the role of overseer or superintendent, which therein embraces a new God-given mantle of leadership for today's Church and her leaders. I heartened ministers, challenged with how to lead during such a tumultuous time, to be careful with online comments and to focus on what they wanted to be known for, not what they might be against or the particulars giving them the most concern. Sometimes judgments made too quickly or snap decisions have a way of becoming unfastened. We should use more caution and discernment, especially in trying times.

The longer this pandemic challenged societal freedoms and concerns of religious liberties the more challenged were God's leaders in offering the Father's character and heart of unity for all concerned. I encouraged ministers that each should strive in every way possible to keep the unity of the faith for the purpose and the witness we portray.

> "Wisdom is more precious than rubies and nothing you desire can compare with her" (Proverbs 3:15, NIV).

God appeared to Solomon and gave him the opportunity to ask for anything he desired. What did Solomon desire more than all else? Wisdom. Not gold or long life, or to be right on a topic of societal concern, but wisdom. Wisdom is supreme. It is great to have knowledge, but more valuable is to have the wisdom to apply it.

Not many weeks had passed of the C19 international crisis, when I encouraged ministers with this.

> I encourage you to pause before post. I encourage you to consider your public witness with your social media. I encourage you to realize while you may be immovable about a subject, with every right to be so, to whom much is given much is required that we might not become harmful to the body of Christ and a point of disunity, rather than focused purpose. Use maturity, developed wisdom, and reliable responsibility in your leadership. A colleague in a nearby state wrote wisely, "remain vigilant in (our) service to the Lord and open to the leading of His Spirit until such time as public gatherings can be held again. That day is coming, friends, so hang in there!"

Following months of in-home seclusion and a myriad of new-normal routines that came from this century-defining season, how the Church converses, networks, trains, connects, and even worships for the years to come was taken to a new, and in some cases, even fresh, level. Many of these changes may remain for years to come.

COVID-19 and Kindness

Suffering brings both external and internal change in our lives and presents a myriad of opportunities to respond in godly ways. I wrote in the May 2020 "Good News" special edition of the *Kentucky Challenge*, a monthly magazine published by my office:

> This plague has shown us how swiftly our lives can change, how delicate our health can be, and how significant our friends and family are to us. ... And, it's time to ... formulate an action plan ... for your congregation ... and ... for your community. Remember, Jesus didn't call us to 'be' disciples, but to 'make' disciples.

Russian author, Leo Tolstoy, author of *War and Peace*, said around 1860, "Everybody thinks of changing humanity and nobody thinks of changing himself." Possibly, COVID-19 did just that: changed all of us, to some degree. I pray, for the better. Even in the midst of a pandemic, kindness arose.

Forbes Magazine (March 17, 2020) quoted Mr. Rogers, an American Presbyterian minister and iconic television personality from Pittsburgh, Pennsylvania, who created a thirty-three-year series, Mr. Roger's Neighborhood: "Mr. Rogers once said, 'When I was a boy and I would see scary things in the news, my mom would say to me 'Look for the helpers. You will always find people who are helping.'" There was good news that could be found from the season of COVID-19.

> *Suffering brings both external and internal change in our lives and presents a myriad of opportunities to respond in godly ways.*

Companies large and small went out of their way to continue paying employees during this crisis. COVID-19 funds were created from the East coast to the West coast to offer assistance for those most adversely impacted. Coffee shops and restaurants offered complimentary services for medical personal. Zoom.com helped make the world more accessible. Free digital training and resourcing was found readily. Good souls sewed facemasks and mailed them to health care workers. Encouraging patrons gave generous tips to assist restaurant employees. People made hand sanitizer for friends, groups, and networks. Food banks went into overdrive.

Drive-by prayers and meal drop-offs won battles against hunger and discouragement. Neighbors again began calling and checking on people like had not been seen in years. Thank you notes were again showing up on car windshields, front doorknobs, and on front porches. People generously made donations. Some entered blood banks and gave blood. Individuals worked to keep safe distances with social distancing to protect themselves and others from infection or simply stayed home as much as possible to help stem the tide. Corporations like Amazon hired tens of thousands of new employees and gave raises to present workers during COVID-19. Mental health benefits across numerous companies were offered confidentially and free of charge for employees struggling.

Millions of dollars were donated by large corporations for COVID-19 recovery and for hospitals dealing with the crisis. Unlimited sick leave was offered to millions of employees across the nation for those dealing with COVID-19 symptoms. Large corporate CEOs offered their multi-million-dollar annual salaries to help keep employees on the payroll. Eonomists offered encouraging news as to post-COVID-19 recovery for America's financial future.

COVID-19 and Spiritual Hunger

The intimate nature of private worship draws one to the deeper and more revealing things of our lives and of God. Somehow truth unfolds, and the heart of God is discovered.

Numerous days of rain in the Louisville area where I reside filled the spring of 2020. I smile, because ... through it all, I sensed ... rain of a spiritual kind (Isa 45:8). It was a time when it appeared that deep was calling out to deep. Just as rain is a mystery, so too are we faced with the mysteries tied to this remarkable time. A great harvest is ready and awaiting. God is the Creator. I am the created. He is calling. He is the potter. I am the clay. He is molding me. Just like a passage of Scripture I shared at my sister's funeral a few years ago, "No eye has seen, no ear has heard, nor can it be conceived, the things God has planned for His children" (1 Cor 2:9).

> *The intimate nature of private worship draws one to the deeper and more revealing things of our lives and of God.*

While in no way suggesting that the Church's months of being removed from their buildings, or their trajectory to online services and ministries (1) compares to tyrannies endured by a Chinese Church (of which I am completed unqualified to address), or (2) suggests that the U.S. situation is somehow deeply political or much more than a genuine attempt to squelch a viral pandemic that has taken tens of thousands of lives around the globe, I am prompted how decades of law, persecution, discrimination, oppression, and intimidation, primarily moving the Chinese Church underground, triggered and produced a well-spring of revival and Holy Spirit directed life and church growth. Some have said there are now over 100 million believers in China—and all from the underground church. What a privilege it is to be called and to be active in the ministry of the gospel. Lead on, friends.

Jesus said, "I will build my church and the gates of hell shall not prevail against it" (Matt 16:18, KJV).

Looking Ahead

None of us knows what the future will bring, but we know Who will bring the future.

The pandemic led to re-evaluating church trends for the new normal being experienced around the globe. Are we as ministers interested in filling buildings or fulfilling the mandate of reaching the lost? Most agreed there would not be a specific moment when local church attendance returned to pre-pandemic numbers or when what was known and recognized previously would return again. Rather, it would be a measured emergence to the new-norm. COVID added to the declining attendance at local churches. The realization came that the Church would grow and continue (as has been experienced through the ages during trial and tribulations) but that the majority of attendees might not be parking their cars and walking to the brick and mortar building with a steeple. An emphasis on gathering will likely be replaced in years to come with bonding and the building of relationships. Helping people find their tribe is not as complicated as it sounds when you connect them to others in relationship. And, it is likely church attendees will engage from virtual venues, home-based settings, and micro-gatherings more than ever before as we lead into the decades ahead. As the bible instructs that God's people not forsake gathering together (Hebrews 10:25), gathering for worship on the Sabbath will remain paramount. It simply will not all occur in buildings owned by churches. Mission is more important than method. It is time the mission of God become priority once again.

Our lives as believers are in God's hands. The Bible encourages us in Matthew 6:26-27 (NIV) not to worry but to trust in God's loving care no matter what: "Look at the birds of the air; they do not sow or reap or store away in barns, and yet your heavenly Father feeds them. Are you not much more valuable than they? Can any one of you by worrying add a single hour to your life?"

Worrying doesn't stop bad things from occurring, it just freezes you from enjoying the good. Reach for the divine possibilities. Obstacles will cause us to lose focus. Keep your eyes on the prize. Trust in the Lord. We're reminded in Joshua 1:9, "Have I not commanded you? Be strong and courageous. Do not be afraid; do not be discouraged, for the LORD your God will be with you wherever you go" (NIV). And, the Psalmist said (9:10), "Those who know your name trust in you, for you, LORD, have never forsaken those who seek you." (NIV).

A friend recently told me that near-death experiences cause us to refocus. Often the worse thing that can happen to me is the greatest thing that ever happened. Somehow through all we endure or encounter, God knows best and is working His plan in us and for us for His good pleasure. In revival paradigms leaders must become wise to satanic strategy. It is not uncommon that on the backside of the desert the greatest lessons are learned. God either calms the raging storms around you or He will calm you in the midst of yours, your valleys, your facing-the-mountain experiences, and your desert places. Trust Him.

> *Pandemic does not thwart the mission and work of God.*

Revival history offers multiple examples of global and national spiritual revival during and following times of turmoil, disorder, and unrest. Pandemic does not thwart the mission and work of God. Let us continue to walk in kindness, for it is the "kindness of God leads ... to repentance" (Rom 2:4, NASB). And let us hunger for the touch of God's Spirit on our hurting world. Come, Lord Jesus. Come.

Chapter 7

Rapture? Mark of the Beast?

"For the time is coming when people will not endure sound teaching, but having itching ears they will accumulate for themselves teachers to suit their own passions, and will turn away from listening to the truth and wander off into myths"
(2 Timothy 4:3-4, ESV).

It has been said that pulpits are far too silent on such topics in today's culture. To have and seek revival demands it. It's all about the lost, friends. The Lord is willing that none should perish. That's what true revival is all about. Revival is seeing lives changed for all eternity. He is slow to anger, patient in wrath, and merciful to no end. Many over recent generations have dismissed topics such as these as fables or 1800's folklore. But, is it? Faithful bible scholars around the world believe these things to be true. And, so do I.

A day will come when churches will be closed, Christian gatherings will be found illegal, and those spiritual voices will be imprisoned. It's already begun. What was once viewed as mainstream biblical knowledge of eschatological events will be unknown and unheard.

Let's look at this biblical narrative unmatched and incomparable to any other book you've ever read! Scripture gives the reader a masterful description of characters and occurrences. Global conversations during pandemic were often framed by discussions of chaos, international turmoil, economic downturns, spiritual depravity, and more. It was not uncommon to hear church members asking or talking together over coffee about their opinions of end-times days and a final revival that surely would soon come to the earth. As you prepare for revival allow this chapter to spark new interest in topics too often left silent for generations. News broadcasts and print media found the topic germane as the world became obsessed with new vaccines being created that would hopefully protect from the deadly virus pandemic crossing the nations.

> *It's all about the lost, friends. The Lord is willing that none should perish.*

How long has it been since you even thought about the bible's concept of "the rapture" or (if you or your loved ones were to miss that snatching away) "the mark of the beast"? I have always warned people to ready themselves for the rapture. Now, I am compelled that the rapture of the church is sure and soon. Holiness and righteousness is culturally scorned. The many gods of this world are given credence as blinded eyes continue in lifestyles of sin and biblical antithesis. Some say, "What does it matter?" Well, there's a lot of theology in between, but it matters because Heaven is real and so is Hell. Hell is a place of torment (Luke 16:23). Hell lasts forever (Revelation 14:11). There is no escape from Hell (Matthew 25:46). And, what we want all people to understand – they didn't have to go there (2 Peter 3:9). To help people anticipate the glorious rapture of the church we must first be about the Father's business becoming fishers of men.

Years ago I solidified my faith to the bible account of the rapture of the church. I anticipate it could occur at any moment, in the "twinkling of an eye". Put oil in your lamps, friends. Get ready. What a privilege to live during these unprecedented days. A heart of genuine repentance reaps an eternal reward.

As I write this, my mother-in-law, one hundred percent

Italian (her grandparents immigrated from Italy in 1903 and her mother was born in Brazil during that long journey), fights for life on a ventilator in a Louisville hospital critical from Coronavirus complications. I think of how she's impacted my life. Just weeks ago she stood at my Louisville home kitchen stove crafting one of her remarkable pasta meals. I once asked her (Annette Vannucci) what she felt was her most meaningful and poignant thought regarding rapture. She has served the Lord since she was a little girl. She was in church in her mother's womb. She is one of the greatest bible teacher's I have ever heard. Her depth in the Word and in prayer is unparalleled. Without hesitation she responded, "to see the Lord".

The rapture and the second coming of Christ are often confused. They are similar but very separate events. The rapture is when Jesus returns to remove the Church from the earth according to 1 Thessalonians 4:13-18 and 1 Corinthians 15:50-54. Believers who have died will have their bodies resurrected and along with believers still living will meet the Lord in the air. No one knows when it will occur, but it will occur rapidly and without warning. The need to be ready and have one's life in order is so important for us all. The second coming is when Jesus returns to defeat the anti-Christ, destroy evil, and establish His millennial kingdom (according to Revelation 19:1-16).

What are some of the key differences between the rapture and the second coming of Christ? I think it's important to note that the word rapture is not in the bible. The Greek word "parousia" translates as a "snatching away".

At this snatching away of the saints, the rapture, believers meet the Lord in the air. At the second coming, believers return with the Lord to the earth. The second coming occurs after the great tribulation (see the Revelation 19 passage reference above). The rapture occurs before the tribulation (see 1 Thessalonians 5:9 and Revelation 3:10). The rapture delivers believers from the earth (see 1 Thessalonians 4:13f and 5:9). The second coming includes the removal of unbelievers in judgment according to Matthew 24:40-41. And, the rapture will be secret and instant (see 1 Corinthians 15:50f), while the second coming is clearly visible to all (see Revelation 1:7 and Matthew 24:29-30).

Alluding to the great tribulation above, I believe the bible teaches that true believers will not go through this period. Why? The bible says in Revelation 3:10, "Because thou hast kept the word of my patience, I will also keep thee from the hour of temptation which shall come upon all the world..." (KJV). And, the bible says, "God hath not appointed us unto wrath, but unto salvation through Jesus Christ" (1 Thessalonians 5:9, KJV).

I have always found comfort in the promise of God's word that the Lord will descend from heaven and that the dead in Christ would rise first to meet Him in the air. *There are no imposters coming. It is Jesus, Himself.* As I reminisce on the numbers of family and friends who have already passed from this life, I am reminded of the great reunion promised. Take heart, friends. In Christ, you will see your loved ones again!

What about those who aren't serving the Lord at the time of his return for this snatching away? I can't imagine what it would be like living in that time without Christ. The saddest thing in life is a lost soul. And, I heard it said one time, a wasted life.

Relate those matters to bible prophecy. John the Revelator spoke of days that most people cannot imagine. Would you accept a mark that without it you would be unable to buy or sell? Will the nations recognize and identify the mark of the Beast when it occurs? More so, will the Church existing at the time distinguish it? Certainly, in trying times such as during a global pandemic, revival conversation is often directed to the prophetic books of Daniel and Revelation. The previous chapter looked through the lens of COVID-19. During this unique season, conversations about micro-chipping took place both with respect to its political and economic aspects.

Many do not realize that micro-chipping initially began in the late 1990s when experiments with radio-frequency identification

(RFID) implants were carried out in 1998. British scientist, Kevin Warwick, was applauded at the time by global researchers for his ingenuity. His implant was used to open doors, switch on lights, and cause verbal output within a building.

Could it be possible that global citizens over twenty years later could soon be recognized, their medical histories instantly known, banking and financial transactions conducted with a scan, and all pertinent documentations stored within or on their body in some fashion? Is it possible that inadvertently, or at the least unwittingly, COVID-19 set the stage for one's autonomy to be stolen without notice? Is it likewise possible that national and international revival currents were set in motion at the same time?

Politically, socially, anthropologically, and spiritually, the jury is still out on whether COVID-19 could be the initiation season to usher in a one-world currency, one-world government, and one-world system that challenges privacy while being riddled with ethical questions. The digital world we are propelled to engage in brings to question whether or not I actually want my physicians to know *everything* about me with a simple scan of the wand. Also, some are questioning whether the Bible has already spoken of this unique time in the world's history. Well, to some extent, yes, it has, but I'm not so sure it's *this* time in history.

Still, it behooves us to know what Scripture says about such a day to come. We can find solace that though the Bible was written over sixteen centuries by at least forty Spirit-led authors, it carries one principal premise—salvation through faith in Christ alone. The following verses speak to these concerns:

> I saw thrones on which were seated those who had been given authority to judge. And I saw the souls of those who had been beheaded because of their testimony about Jesus and because of the word of God. They had not worshiped the beast or its image and had not received its mark on their foreheads or their hands. They came to life and reigned with Christ a thousand years (Rev 20:4, NIV).

It also forced all people, great and small, rich and poor, free and slave, to receive a mark on their right hands or on their foreheads, so that they could not buy or sell unless they had the mark, which is the name of the beast or the number of its name (Rev 13:16-17, NIV).

Dear children, this is the last hour; and as you have heard that the antichrist is coming, even now many antichrists have come. This is how we know it is the last hour (1 John 2:18, NIV).

What or Who is the Beast?

I offer that the antichrist (the beast) will be the wicked one imposing this mark. Receiving his mark will be the presenting symbol of revering his leadership, as if worshipping him (the beast and choosing him over God). Revelation 13:17 describes the False Prophet's discharge of the mark. Notice a Greek word, *charagma*, used to define the stamping or branding of livestock. The resolve of this mark is to distinguish the possessor as one devoted to the Antichrist. Other accounts in the book of Revelation make it well-defined that genuine believers will refuse this mark (Revelation 20:4), and those who take it are knowledgeably denying God and His gospel (Revelation 14:9-11). It is clear that the mark is not something that people will be tricked into accepting unknowingly innocuously, or unintentionally.

> *The resolve of this mark is to distinguish the possessor as one devoted to the Antichrist.*

The Apostle Paul addresses the Thessalonians with reassuring and heartening discourse when he offers his only reference to this topic in 2 Thessalonians: "Concerning the coming of our Lord Jesus Christ..." (2:1, NIV). First-century Christians (former Greeks in this passage who received Paul's words of God's grace and peace) faced faith with anticipation and found trials that would follow. Nonetheless, Paul made it clear to them that they had both a life to live and a future ahead to embrace. Remember, the triumph belongs to the Lord, and those following Him:

> Don't let anyone deceive you in any way, for that day will not come until the rebellion occurs and the man of lawlessness is revealed, the man doomed to destruction. He will oppose and will exalt himself over everything that is called God or is worshipped, so that he sets himself up in God's temple, proclaiming himself to be God (2 Thessalonians 2:3-4, NIV).

The mark of the beast will be placed on the right hand or on the forehead (Rev 13:16), sanctioning individuals who accept it to either "purchase or sell." Scripture contends that no one can do so without having accepted the mark (Rev 13:17).

It will be a requirement—perhaps by decree—to acquire the mark with grave penalties for those who reject. Everyone—rich or lowly, old or youthful, free or imprisoned—will be mandated to get this mark (Rev 13:16).

Do I Believe That ~ Literally?

Some may be thinking, does this author literally believe the Bible—word for word? And, my answer is, with a pause, so you can ponder my response, yes, and no. In nearly thirty-five years of ministry, I have had the privilege to dispel a number of confused individuals as to what Christians actually do believe. When asked if I believe the Bible in a literal sense, then no, I do not. To which, many of you are gasping at the moment, and others are pleasantly relieved. However, I make it clear to all that I fully believe everything in the Bible as holy and true.

If you ask me to literally accept every verse of the Bible as it is written, then you are asking me to believe that Jesus is a door, that He is a rock, or that He is a lamb or a lion, or a rose or a lily. I don't know one serious student of the Bible who would say they believed Jesus was a flower growing in a field, or an animal grazing on a hill or running through sub-Saharan grasslands. If you question whether I categorically believe the Bible, then my answer is an emphatic and wholly convinced, yes. So, while I may not take a literal view of the Bible, I fully embrace a literalist approach to Scripture. Literalism does not deny that parables, metaphors, and symbols occur in the Bible. A literal acceptance of Scripture trusts contextual analyses grounded on seeming authorial objective and purpose.

So, in the case of the mark of the beast, do I believe it to be a literal mark of some sort that is implanted or emblazoned on an individual that will grant certain information and rights as the Bible says? Yes, I do, and I am fully convinced that a follower of Jesus Christ should not receive the mark (whatever it is, or in whatever fashion it occurs and is required, when that day arrives). With that said, let's discuss some of it in context to foundational Scripture germane to the topic.

Do Not Receive the Mark

Let me make it clear: As I alluded previously in this chapter, do not receive the mark. The world will not think of it as a mark "of the beast," but rather a mark of submission and cultural acceptance, a way of doing business, and instant access to information that accepts and agrees to a new norm of societal efficiency and cooperation. After all, everyone is getting it.

Further, it is imperative to remember that this "mark" cannot be acquired by chance. It's not something one can accidentally receive. Dr. David Thomas, New Testament theologian and former professor at Northwest University in Kirkland, WA, remarked in conversation with me on the topic: "This doesn't at all mean people aren't being deceived, but it does mean that their action in receiving it is deliberate acquiescence."

> *The world will not think of it as a mark "of the beast," but rather a mark of submission.*

What Happens to a Person Who Accepts This Mark?

The mark of the beast is portrayed in Scripture at its ultimate, core, and primary level as counterfeit. It was first God's divine handiwork to offer His mark of ownership upon humankind. In speaking with Dr. Thomas, he added of this concept, "It appears first in Ezekiel 9:4ff, is repeated in Revelation 7:1ff, then again in Revelation 14:1ff." Satan counterfeits the mark of God. When the end of time occurs, apocalyptic framework offers that everyone will bear a mark, a name on the forehead. It's simply a matter of *which* label a given individual will assume. I am reminded of *tefllin* or phylacteries (derived from the Greek *phylakterion*, meaning amulet), a set of small black leather boxes containing scrolls of parchment inscribed with verses from the Torah worn about the forehead in morning and evening prayers. My prayer is that you will be found faithful.

> A third angel followed them and said in a loud voice: 'If anyone worships the beast and its image and receives its mark on their forehead or on their hand, they, too, will drink the wine of God's fury, which has been poured full strength into the cup of his wrath. They will be tormented with burning sulfur in the presence of the holy angels and of the Lamb. And the smoke of their torment will rise forever and ever. There will be no rest day or night for those who worship the beast and its image, or for anyone who receives the mark of its name'" (Rev 14:9-11, NIV).

The beast will deceive people of the world by performing spectacular miracles, such as making fire come down from heaven (Rev 13:13-14) and will come posturing as the Messiah. The planet will be in awe and thoughtlessly worship the beast, thinking he is a savior. Christian, beware. Do not be deceived.

Calvary/Golgotha[107] and Why to Avoid the Mark

Christ died on the Cross at Calvary taking on himself the sin of all people of the world. I have walked the Via Dolorosa in the Old City of Jerusalem. I have gazed upon the locations considered the hill of Mount Calvary. I have stood at the entrance to an empty tomb. Eternal life, forgiveness of humanity's sin, and one's personal salvation are found only in Jesus and His substitutionary work on that Cross.

By accepting in one's heart what Jesus did at Calvary, the believer is adopted into God's family. It is God who lives in you, who works in you, and who will keep you firm to the end. You are a child of God. You are not a child of the evil one or the beast. If you are truly a child of God, then you will not get the mark. If challenged unto death, followers of Jesus Christ will not deny their faith or their trust in God's holy Word. The test of whether one accepts the mark of the beast will expose who is a true Christian. It will distinguish Christians from those merely calling themselves Christian but who are actually insincere in their faith. Further, God declares that if any of His followers receive the mark, they will be destined for "the Lake of Fire and Brimstone" (Revelation 20:10) where the antichrist, the false prophet, and Satan will be cast.

Christian suffering has occurred since the first century. Today, we continue to live in our own period of martyrdom as we receive repeated news of global terrorism, Christians murdered for their faith, and more. That is today. What about tomorrow? Believers faced with the ordeal of living in the day when the mark of the beast comes upon the earth will be confronted with the unthinkable choice of offering their lives for the Lord.

Christian suffering has occurred since the first century.

We do not belong in this world. We've been chosen out of it (John 15:19). All of us know what it is like to be in a home that is not our own. Those blessed have tables and chairs, beds, and couches, food, and comforts, but when we are in someone else's house, those things are not our own. We don't always feel welcome here on earth. This isn't our home. Yet, in that hour, several will become weak and in panic suppose, "This could not be the mark I've heard about" and consent to it as it comes.

The sad reality is that there are many immovable individuals who will not take God's free gift of eternal salvation the first time around, and they will suffer extreme consequences for not doing so.

There is good news, though. The Bible tells us of a gathering of God's people before the antichrist has the opportunity to deceive the masses. This event is referred to as the "Rapture" of the Church. It will entail God alerting His people, protecting, and sparing as many as have believed, ushering them to heaven before the turmoil overcomes those on earth.

> For the Lord Himself will descend from heaven with a shout, with the voice of an archangel, and with the trumpet of God. And, the dead in Christ will rise first. Then we who are alive and remain shall be caught up together with them in the clouds to meet the Lord in the air. And thus we shall always be with the Lord (1 Thess 4:16-17, NKJV).

> Because you have kept my command to persevere, I also will keep you from the hour of trial which shall come upon the whole world, to test those who dwell on the earth (Rev 3:10, NKJV).

The following verse could be a literal interpretation of Jesus keeping His Body of believers living at this time out of the hands of the Antichrist:

> Watch therefore, and pray always that you may be counted worthy to escape all these things that will come to pass, and to stand before the Son of Man (Luke 21:36, NKJV).

The world continues to change before our eyes. You may experience success or failures, health or sickness, healing or the death of loved ones, financial gain or loss, or relocation to a better or less desired place. Through whatever circumstances that come remain faithful to the Holy One. Remember, Jesus is our hope, and our salvation.

> "For who shall separate us from the love of Christ? Shall trouble or hardship or persecution or famine or nakedness or danger or sword? No, in all these things we are more than conquerors through Him who loved us. For I am convinced that neither death nor life, neither angels nor demons, neither the present nor the future, nor any powers, neither height nor depth, nor anything else in all creation will be able to separate us from the love of God that is in Christ Jesus our Lord"
>
> (Romans 8:35f, NIV).

Chapter 8

An Appointed Time

> *"For God so loved the world, that he gave his only Son, that whoever believes in him should not perish but have eternal life. For God did not send his Son into the world to condemn the world, but in order that the world might be saved through him"* (John 3:16-17, ESV).

Ben

I sat one mid-Spring morning, black coffee in hand. It was a strong and aromatic beginning to the day. This particular morning it seemed as though every sip of coffee brought to my mind something from deep within. Chris Tomlin's worship melodies softly streamed on my smart phone's app as I took in the impressive 6:30 a.m. sunrise from the east in our small suburb of Louisville, Kentucky. My eyes absorbed the overgrowth and wooded parcel that just weeks prior had been cleared by Ben.

The day before, I had stood first with Ben's father, then his mother and siblings, in a cold back room of a funeral home, looking at Ben's still, silenced body, prepared for his final moments, as it lay on the metal table. With no opportunity to say goodbyes or give final hugs of love and affection, closure was necessary—even essential.

Revival, Racism & Rapture

Does our Father in heaven truly love us? Does the Holy Spirit move among us? He does. Does our God intend to dwell with us in these darkest of days? He does. Is anyone able to open the scroll (Rev 5:2-3)? He is. Will they or we ever truly understand such loss this side of heaven? Doubtful. Will we continue to praise the Lord and lean on His promises through it all? We will.

It was said he didn't see it. It was assumed he didn't feel it. The large tree Ben had cut just seconds before to be felled, snapped before he could move. Another company would now handle the bucking. The practice of cutting a tree into serviceable sizes is called bucking. Bucking regularly occurs as a tree is being limbed, such as when the branches of the crown are to be recycled as firewood. The lone secondary, one sole worker along Ben's side to assist, heard two sounds: snap, thud. Ben was caught beneath the enormous timber, lifeless. What could describe such sudden loss? It was an act shockingly rigid, dreadful, violent, unseen, pitilessly cruel, immediate, certain, painless, honorable only in that a man died doing what he loved.

For years, Ben, a bright and promising university economics graduate had relished every minute of operating the small local company manicuring lawns or wielding his chain saw as a local lumberjack. He loved his work. He was well known and respected for his skills. He used his degree and turned it into a profitable local business. It was a lovely ride that was ended far too soon.

The Bible says, "all the days ordained for me were written in your book before one of them came to be" (Ps 139:16, NIV). That explains, God knows exactly when, where, and how we will die. The Psalmist David declared in Psalm 31:15, "My times are in your hand" (NIV). There are shifts in life, seasons that end, and seasons of new beginnings. Solomon, acknowledged as the wisest man on earth, understood this concept (Eccl 3:1-8) realizing that

An Appointed Time

time travels without us purely because it solely belongs to God, himself. Solomon surrendered his life to the sovereign Creator, humbly receiving that he could not fully comprehend or control various occurrences of his life.

I did not know whether the voicemail of genuine condolences and prayer left on the recording for the family before hanging up the phone would be heard, or meaningful in anyway. I simply offered what one could—care, concern, and prayer. Leonard Ravenhill says in his revival classic, *Why Revival Tarries*, that there are three individuals in each of us. Each person has a perception of what we think we're like. Of course, other people see what they perceive. And, the truth is the persona that God knows we are. This day, I was hoping for God to transform who Dennis (Ben's father) knew me to be into one called of God and to His purposes. The subsequent call a day later asking if I could fit in an appointment to meet the family in fifteen minutes at a local funeral home was an immediate, "Yes," with the sense that God might be introducing a door only He could devise. What's the chance that I, a mere customer one day, an acquaintance by business, would the next day be granted a fifteen minute notice to be the sole clergy called upon to help in such time of need?

We've often hoped the sentiments were true from James' Taylor's hit, "You've got a friend; winter, spring, summer, or fall, all you have to do is call." Dennis was a former Navy pilot now civilian, having retired from his career as a United Parcel Service (UPS) pilot. He relocated years earlier to the company hub in Louisville, Kentucky and was fortunate with means far beyond what any average family would experience (though no one would have ever known it). Dennis had a welcoming and certain humility about him uncommon in society today. At this moment, Dennis was quite simply a hurting father who had called in a friend's offer.

> *I had witnessed the most daunting afternoon in a family's life.*

This father later admitted that the guys in Ben's business

initially thought I was a "jackass" (to use his term) because I had been so picky through the years with how I wanted my lawn to look when they would mow it. Years ago, I mowed lawns, as did many North American high school or middle school students. I learned early the simple tricks to keep one's lawn looking pristine. This day responding to Dennis' call—with a lawn as our common ground, and within an hour—I had witnessed the most daunting afternoon in a family's life.

When life gets blurry, we have to adjust our focus. Just maybe, that's what revival is all about. As discerned, the Lord granted the occasion for me to personally yet briefly share with Dennis and pray a prayer of salvation with him as he left the emptiness of the mortuary's back room. In his pain, I pointed him to Jesus, the only true Healer.

Only heaven's timetable comprehends these eternal moments set in order for both father and son. In 2 Timothy 4:2 the Apostle Paul prompts Timothy to be instant (ready) in season and out of season. Paul was telling Christ's followers to stand prepared in moments of opportunity, persuaded that God's Word is the commanding capital that transforms lives.

God's love constrains me to seek the anguished and console the hurting. To save a heart that finds itself lost is the prayer of any revivalist. Discipleship becomes more than a program. Friends don't let friends go to hell. Discipleship is personally sharing Christ as doors are opened for seeking hearts to encounter His presence.

> *To save a heart that finds itself lost is the prayer of any revivalist.*

Over the weeks to follow multiple text messages and phone calls were exchanged. I sent Dennis Scripture verses, dozens of personal growth and reflection discipling materials. I followed up his inquiry sending him names of counseling organizations, psychologists, and psychiatrists for potential reference that his family might need in days to come dealing with their ongoing grief. My wife and I visited and sat on his peaceful front porch to spend time with our new friend and his family in their darkest

An Appointed Time

hours.

Revival grows in the hearts of men and women who are introduced to and rest in God's abiding presence. What does that passage from the Psalms really mean? "Be still, and know that I am God (Psalm 46:10, KJV). Stop talking. Turn off your cell phones. You don't have to react or respond to every post that frustrates your spirit. Listen more. Argue less. Don't question everyone or everything. Just, be still. Let doubt flee. Be certain. Live in faith. You don't need to second-guess yourself when you're heart is content in God's promises. Simply, know. The Great I Am is Almighty. God has this problem you face covered. He is love. He is King. And, He is life and hope.

Drew

Weeks later, early in the summer of 2020, I was standing in the driveway of my suburban Louisville home talking with a contract manager of a large home remodel project we'd undergone in previous months. His name was Jeremy. Oddly enough, we stood talking only a half-dozen steps from a location, new and replacement grass still growing, where Ben had months earlier cut down and removed an overgrown tree. I had known from one of our first encounters nearly six months earlier that this contractor's six-year-old son had been hospitalized and undergone chemotherapy treatments for a rare form of cancer.

I listened intently as this father shared briefly how COVID-19 had impacted his business and family life, yet how well his son seemed to be doing amidst it all. He realized that every three-month doctor visit continues to give them the uneasy feeling of "what if...?" Jeremy conceded that he and his family had found through this cancerous ordeal a way to somehow draw closer to understanding the things of God. He felt no fault against God for his son's cancer, recognizing that there is a reason for all things, though rarely understood.

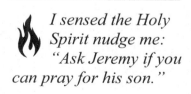

I sensed the Holy Spirit nudge me: "Ask Jeremy if you can pray for his son."

I listened. Could it be that was a key to opening revival?

Then, finding a suitable time to comment, I shared briefly about recent happenings regarding Ben and his father, Dennis, mentioning how that father likewise was finding solace in the midst of things that could not be blamed on God yet were challenging to comprehend. Jeremy listened intently as I shared of another's heartbreak and journey to recovery.

Then, as quickly as I had received a call from Dennis weeks earlier to meet him in fifteen minutes (in a moment that began a new journey for both him and me), I sensed the Holy Spirit nudge me: "Ask Jeremy if you can pray for his son."

So I did.

"Jeremy, what is your son's name? And, would you mind if I prayed for him?"

Instantly, he responded, "Drew. And, yes, please, thank you."

I immediately—and quite simply—began to pray for Drew, then for his mom and dad, all while standing in the driveway of my home.

The Lord can break down the weight of mountains and remove great divides. Tears filled Jeremy's eyes as I gently closed the prayer, "...in Jesus's name. Amen."

He was so grateful, saying before he left, "What a great way to start a Friday; thank you."

What if I had been worried about Jeremy's opinion of me? People too often worry about someone else's opinion. I heard it said once that a tiger doesn't lose sleep over the opinion of his next meal. The world is changed by example, not opinion. What if I had been worried that he would be offended if I brought up prayer or faith? If you want to make it easier to be happy, make it harder to be offended. So, I simply cared. I cared about what was closest to Jeremy's heart—Drew. Unplug your worries, and reboot your soul.

The world is changed by example, not opinion.

An Appointed Time

I did not know at the time I spoke to Jeremy that day what my wife told me after this encounter. Just two weeks prior she had been thinking – praying - of how sweet it would be if the Lord would open a door for me to pray with Jeremy, our contractor. Then, just like that, Chris Tomlin's words of "how sweet it is to be loved by Jesus" rang in my heart. I heard it 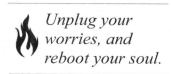 said once, "No burden is too heavy when carried with love." It's easy to confess, I'm not always at my best. But in those times of worry or questioning your move, the Lord is your strength in the moments you're weak. He'll keep giving you grace to proceed and breath life to those in need.

Unplug your worries, and reboot your soul.

Simply Announce the Good News

Born in London, England in 1921, John Stott became a noted leader in the worldwide evangelical movement. He was an English Anglican priest and theologian and one of the principal authors of the Lausanne Covenant in 1974. *Time* magazine ranked Stott among the 100 most influential people in the world in 2005. I had the privilege to hear Stott speak in my early seminary days at Asbury Theological Seminary in Wilmore, Kentucky in the mid 1980s. Stott said, "To evangelize does not mean to win converts ... but simply to announce the good news, irrespective of the results."

I was a small child of about six when I accompanied my parents to a large stadium crusade in Knoxville, Tennessee held by famed evangelist to nations and presidents, Billy Graham. It was only months prior to my parents' divorce on their twenty-fifth wedding anniversary. Graham was noted as saying, "We are the Bibles the world is reading; we are the creeds the world is needing; we are the sermons the world is heeding." Our family had their fair share of storms, but I am living proof that the power of the Lord never goes out in the raging storm. Much like Peter, I have learned that stepping onto a turbulent sea is not a move of logic but desperate trust in Him. Who can fathom?

As I write these words Easter Sunday is just days away. Easter is the most celebrated and joyous day on the Christian calendar. I'm grateful that dark Fridays for all of us have a resurrection Sunday upcoming! Recently a friend offered encouragement to me from Mark 15:21. It is there we're told Roman soldiers compelled Simon of Cyrene to carry Jesus' cross when he could carry it no more.

Simon was the last one to help Jesus. He was a known man of business. An olive farmer from the South Aegean Sea, today it is believed that his city is a Greek colony well recognized for turquois blue waters, stunning sunsets, and the whitewashed architecture (to offset the high noon heat from the sun) of houses clinging to cliffs overlooking such seafaring beauty. Santorini, or Cyrene, was a coastal town of Libya at the time of Simon's face-to-face encounter with a battered and physically weary Jesus on the Via Dolorosa. Simon was nearly 650 miles from his home when he met Jesus that day on a narrow Jerusalem street. I have walked the Via Dolorosa. It will forever be in my mind. As a processional route in the Old City of Jerusalem, it is notably believed to be the path that Jesus walked – and stumbled - on the approach to his crucifixion. The winding route from the former Antonia Fortress to the Church of the Holy Sepulchre — a distance of about 600 metres — is a renowned location of Christian pilgrimage.

Mark identified Simon by name in this passage. Mark also identified his sons, Alexander and Rufus. Somehow, I marvel that his face-to-face encounter with Jesus that day made an impression that would never leave his heart or his spirit. With some exploring, I learned Simon was eventually consecrated as the first Bishop of the current Archdiocese of Avignon. Both his sons became missionaries and were also likely known to Mark's audience, which gives credence to why Mark would list them by name. Simon was ultimately martyred by crucifixion in 100 AD. That day while in Jerusalem (likely on business), Simon had a direct encounter with Jesus of Nazareth on his way to death. Weakened, Jesus could no longer carry his own cross. Each of us is summoned to carry His cross. And, as Paul told the Galatians,

An Appointed Time

bearing one another's burdens fulfills the law of Christ (Galatians 6:2). Everyone has a cross to bear. Be discerning. Be sensitive. Be aware. Be willing to bear the cross - his and theirs. Every prayer you've prayed for one in distress, battered by cancer, or burdened by the heaviest of loads is your carrying the cross for them when they may have carried it as far as they could go. God sees. God knows. God weighs it all in His balances as the righteous Judge and King.

I was in my thirties when I first read works by Eugene Peterson. Peterson spoke of how Christians don't simply learn or study Scripture. He taught that people assimilate God's word. Somehow, people take it into their lives in unique ways that turn into exploits of love, drinks of cold water, global missions, healing and evangelism and justice in Jesus' name, hands raised in adoration of the Father, feet washed in company with the Son.

Maybe it's time churches today return to the streets with community servanthood. Years ago, I played (trumpet, flugelhorn, and vocals) inspirational music in a Contemporary Christian band. The band's name was *Street Life*. It was old Christian standards coupled with a genre of modern popular music lyrically focused on matters concerned with the Christian faith. We would perform (minister) in various cities on street corners, at festivals, or for churches. It appears today the efforts of street ministry have faded. But, the power of a glass of cold water has not lost its influence.

Who doesn't like to be given an icy soda on a scorching day? For the Christian this would be low-risk and an easy task of caring about "a neighbor". A minor act of kindheartedness prods one closer to God, often in thoughtful and reflective ways. Then you hear the person respond, "I can't believe this is free. Thank you!" The beauty of high-grace is found through that simple act.

Servant evangelism links individuals to others in ordinary ways. They are relaxed, low-risk, and high-grace ways. Kindness builds bridges so others can experience the love of Christ in tangible and understandable ways.

While you may not have to experience a tragedy such as Ben's passing or the concern of a child's cancer, as mentioned above, needs are all around you at all times. People are hurting. Hearts need mending. Words are scattered, thoughts are empty, and never have some felt so low before. At times the walk is lonely, the climb is filled with pain. The simple need of someone to care encompasses us all.

What are practical ways you or your church team could make a difference? How about providing a booth of complimentary regular or decaf coffee (or hot chocolate) at the local soccer fields on a crisp Saturday morning? You can give away iced bottles of water on hot days at your local softball fields. I once heard of a church who purchased large quantities of inexpensive sunglasses ($.50 or $1.00 each) and attended sporting events each weekend simply to let their church bless the community attendees. What if your church surprised local businesses and brought a large basket of treats with a note attached of how you appreciate their work and their heart for the community you love? I'm not much of a golfer. I always wished I were. Typically any day I swing the clubs, I lose three or four golf balls. You could imprint your ministry's name or an encouraging message on golf balls or tees (unexpectedly inexpensive) and make your way to the local course. You'll make a difference and an impact. There are thousands of ways to make a difference. Allow the creativity of the Holy Spirit to work though you. Then, be obedient.

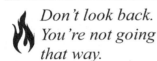

Don't look back. You're not going that way.

I pray for discernment that I might know the moment I am to offer some hurting soul their day's instant and in-season word. The Enneagram test reveals which of 9 personality types fits you best. I'm a classic 2, THE HELPER.

Quite possibly the Lord may call me to carry their cross for them as they can carry it no more. God comes down from heaven to restore lives. Sometimes he uses you and me. Simon of Cyrene carried the cross of Jesus. Yet, it was Simon who was transformed. The Lord is faithful and true. There is an appointed time for all things. Will you be ready? Don't look back. You're not going that way.

Chapter 9

Race Relations (2020)

"For there is no distinction between Jew and Greek; for the same Lord is Lord of all, bestowing his riches on all who call on him"
(Romans 10:12, ESV).

We need to start talking about race. Revival reveals the hope of the eternal. Every knee, every tongue, every tribe, every ethnicity, every race, every color – equal in His sight and created in His image – realize the diverse promises of God. We are called to go and make disciples of all nations (Matthew 28:19). The Psalmist said God rules over all nations (Psalm 22:28). Daniel 7:13-14 speaks to men of every nation serving the Lord Most High. I interpret that as men and women of every color and of every language. In the King James Version of the Bible, a customary version for much of America, the word *nation* appears 145 times. The word *nations* surface 336 times. What happened to the world? What happened to America that caused such ignorance and flagrant abhorrence based solely upon race?

Discrimination, prejudice, bigotry, intolerance, xenophobia, bias, stereotyping, racism—each are words describing attitudes and actions related to race and ethnicity that have characterized the raw emotion and cultural fragmentation of United States citizens throughout its history—but certainly in the trying days of 2020.

In the face of seeing afresh the pain of racial injustice, some well-meaning individuals or groups may offer statements intended for healing but find certain words perceived or interpreted differently than intended.

To respond to the cry, "black lives matter," with the phrase, "all lives matter" may to a white person seem to make total sense in advocating the universal value of all persons. However, in a time when people of color are in great pain from repeated racist traumas such as the senseless murders of Ahmaud Arbery, George Floyd, Breonna Taylor, and so many others, blacks need to know that whites care that *their* particular house is on *fire*, not just that *all houses on the block* matter.

To complicate the issue, the organization "Black Lives Matter," while at times advocating for justice and reform, holds certain views that many people (Christians in particular) who would otherwise support caring for all people would hesitate to embrace. This has often resulted in Anglo citizens or whites backing away publicly from using the terminology, "black lives matter."

The fact remains (for this discussion) that black individuals (many who are my friends) need and deserve love, acceptance, fair treatment, and acknowledgment by whites with respect to past wrongs against them as a people (both past and present).

In these crucial days, it is prudent that leaders address matters of the heart. Systemic racism has beleaguered the United States since the early days of colonialism. Racism has shaped black experiences and white experiences, minority experiences and majority experiences. It has shaped all our experiences. But it does not define us.

During these latest rounds of racial riots and tensions, historic statues of once-revered Confederate leaders were destroyed, removed, or toppled because of the realization that racist history lessons and symbols could be forgotten and ignored no longer.

Race Relations (2020)

America's clergy is once again reexamining its theology and filling its pulpits with messages of life, liberty, and the pursuit of happiness. We must continue to find ways to train and disciple the next generation, lest we repeat the mistakes of the past and lose the opportunity to pursue unity and prosperity for all.

The word race is from a Greek word, *agon*. Our English vernacular for the word *agony* finds its origin in this word. The race set before us can at times be arduous and agonizing—confusing, frustrating, heartbreaking, tormenting, discouraging, distressing, even unbearable. It is no walk in the park. Hebrews 12:1 reminds us to run the race before us and never give up. We must endure to the end and bring healing and unity to our land—maybe for the first time ever. I believe it accomplishable. Negative and negating messages cripple generations. Achievement ideologies empower millions to escape the dearth of destructive lessons. My father taught me to work hard (harder than it appeared others around me were giving), learn from my mistakes, take personal responsibility for my faults and failures, and commit my ways to the Lord. In so, He would direct my steps for healing and victorious living. Today's society needs that healing. In light of our topic, I prayed.

In these crucial days, it is prudent that leaders address matters of the heart.

For my part, I began with crafting the following public and personal statement as a denominational leader for those who have ears to hear. This statement was written just days after the May 25, 2020 murder of George Perry Floyd, Jr., an African American man killed when a white police officer knelt on his neck for a period of 8 minutes and 46 seconds during an arrest for allegedly using a counterfeit $20 in Minneapolis, MN. Few leaders and few pastors were commenting publicly. Few, if any, denominational leaders were addressing the horrors being relived in the United States at the time.

As may have already been mentioned, I presently live in Louisville, Kentucky. Riots became commonplace during this chaos.

Today, as I write, national news wraps up the jury trial of Derek Chauvin, the former Minneapolis police officer charged with murder and manslaughter (accused of killing the unarmed black man, George Floyd). It appeared not a matter of simple justice but of accountability. It was not about system reform. Societal transformation is needed. I can only imagine what it was like in that jury room. The bench of twelve (five men and seven women) deliberated for four hours the first day and offered their verdict after further deliberations on the second. They were sequestered from the public during their discussions. Thousands of protestors have lined Minneapolis and other American streets awaiting this judgment.

Derek Chauvin was found guilty on three counts; second-degree murder, third-degree murder, and second-degree manslaughter. Statutory Maximum sentences could reach 40 years for count one, 25 years for count two, and up to 10 years for count three. He was handcuffed leaving the courtroom for the first time and taken to jail. The George Perry Floyd, Jr. legal team (civil rights leader, and the Rev. Al Sharpton) said following the jury's announcements that "they do not celebrate a man going to jail, as they'd rather have George Floyd alive." The prosecution called 38 people to testify during the month-long trial.

With all that said, if America needs anything today, the nation needs a touch of God. The nation needs unity. Unity is good. Harmony is better. During racially challenged days, weeks, months, and years allies remained critical to reach across dividing boundaries of racism and prejudice. Words of affirmation, care, equality, and support were (and are) needed to bring healing and peace amidst these tumultuous storms.

No doubt the words selected at the time, which have been left for you, the reader, as I initially couched them, could have been and I would further say, should have been re-worded and re-worked if I were to be writing it today. Now, after that moment in our nation's history, I would perhaps propose some of the points differently. But, for honesty and integrity to show the rawness of my heart to the complications at the time, my words have remained as initially presented.

PERSONAL STATEMENT of the KENTUCKY ASSEMBLIES OF GOD NETWORK PASTOR AND SUPERINTENDENT REGARDING INJUSTICE AND RACE RELATIONS

Original Publish Date, June 3, 2020

Suddenly, it seemed as though Coronavirus was a passing concern amidst intense national turmoil regarding race relations. Genuine revival is needed today more than at any other time in modern history.

No words seem to ease pain. It has taken me a week to process even enough of my own grief to offer a public statement. Silence is wrong, but discerning and processing the voice of the Father is heavenly in moments like this.

That heaviness overwhelms people to the point of tears. Friends, Black and Anglo, Hispanic, bi-racial, and minority multi-cultural families, deal with a myriad of emotions, as expected, from anger to brokenness in prayers for their own children's safety growing up in such an unsettled time. Fear and apprehension characterize every day of their lives because of the God-given color of their skin.

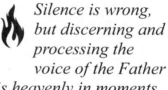

Silence is wrong, but discerning and processing the voice of the Father is heavenly in moments like this.

Walter J. Hollenweger penned the Foreword to Ian MacRobert's 1988 work, *The Black Roots and White Racism of Early Pentecostalism in the USA*. In it, Hollenweger writes:

> Black spirituality in Pentecostalism is evidenced by scores of black hymn-writers and evangelists and above all by William J. Seymour (1870-1922) a son of former slaves from Centerville, Louisiana. Seymour taught himself to read and

write and was for a time a student of Charles Fox Parham's Pentecostal Bible School in Topeka, Kansas (1873-1929), often described as a pioneer of pentecostalism, who was also a sympathizer of the Ku Klux Klan and therefore he excluded Seymour from his Bible classes. Seymour was allowed only to listen outside the classroom through the half-open door. In the face of constant humiliation, Seymour became an apostle of reconciliation ... that ... led to the revival in Los Angeles which most Pentecostal historians believe to be the cradle of Pentecostalism.

On May 25, 2020, George Floyd, a forty-six-year-old unarmed black man in Minneapolis died after a police officer knelt with full body weight on his neck for nearly nine minutes while he cried out, "I can't breathe." Mr. Floyd was arrested for allegedly buying cigarettes with a counterfeit $20 bill.

Just a twenty-minute drive from my home in a Louisville suburb, Breonna Taylor was shot and killed in her apartment during a police raid gone wrong. Ahmaud Arbery was jogging on a South Georgia roadway when he was chased by two gunmen and a third man who was videoing the ordeal. Ahmaud died in that attack to a point blank gunshot wound.

Unfortunately, the rising anger of Summer 2020 is not something only of recent weeks. These murderous atrocities follow the horrible, long line of victims, including

- Seventeen-year-old, unarmed, Trayvon Martin, visiting relatives in a Sanford, Florida neighborhood in February, 2012 and fatally shot just seventy yards from the back door of the townhouse where he was staying.
- Eric Garner (44), killed in a Staten Island, New York incident in the summer of 2014.
- Eighteen-year-old Michael Brown, shot in August of 2014 in a St. Louis suburb (Ferguson, MO).
- Philando Castile (32) who in a St. Paul suburb took five bullets at close range while in his car in the summer of 2016.

The list of names could continue for seemingly an eternity, as citizens of color experience racism recurrently.

Race Relations (2020)

It is not enough to simply say I am opposed to racism. Words must be backed up with actions. I have learned that we don't have to say things perfectly; I simply need to have the conversation.

Begin there.

What am I doing to make a difference? How am I living my life with and among my friends and community? Am I truly standing up for the injustices around me? I can say, "I am sorry." I can say, "I grieve with you." I can say, "I am thankful my minority friends are my friends." Do I genuinely let my voice be heard? I don't want to be blind to what's happening around me. Have I stopped to check in on my Black or minority friends to ask how they're feeling or how they're doing amidst this chaos?

It is not enough to simply say I am opposed to racism. Words must be backed up with actions.

People are enraged, scared, and confused. Could this be the moment that changes a society? Could this be the hour that finally turns the corner for America and the nations of the world in the battle against injustice, racism, and bigotry?

As churches were re-opening for in-person services because of COVID-19, yet at 33 percent capacity and with social distancing regulations, Pentecost Sunday, May 31, 2020, was welcomed with a Louisville-crisp Sunday morning and sunny skies. The beauty of that day did not squelch the new concerns plaguing cities across America. The night before, Louisville mayor, Greg Fischer, had enacted a citywide curfew from 9 p.m. until 6 a.m. to avoid further riot destruction and death. The Thursday previous, seven people had been shot in those Louisville demonstrations. Other cities across the land were experiencing the same. At the midnight hour of this Pentecost Sunday in Louisville, riots led to more shots fired and the killing of yet another individual.

It was with power that the Spirit moved upon the face of the waters (Gen 1:2), and at moments in our spiritual journey, when sometimes waters have been deep, many of you, like myself, have been pricked in our hearts to cry out, "What shall we do?" (Acts 2:37). The abiding presence of the Holy Spirit is my forever Comforter (John 14:16-17). He glorifies Jesus (John 16:14) and empowers people for witness (Acts 1:8). The Scripture authors spoke under unction of the Holy Spirit (2 Pet 1:21), and in those times of my spiritual walk when I need a reminder, it is the Holy Spirit's affirmation to me that I am—though broken and needy—redeemed by Christ and a child of God (Rom 8:16). It is Pentecost—the passion, dedication, and burning desire to preach Good News with unction and conviction—that will bring Christ's healing and redeeming story to the hearts of people before His imminent return. It is within this redemption story revival fires are flamed.

Recent happenings throughout the United States remind us of how far we have yet to go in reaching the mark. This is not a black and white issue. It's a right and wrong issue. I have stood at the locations in Los Angeles where the faithful African-American, Rev. William Seymour (fresh from his unfortunate hallway stoop to be able to overhear the Charles Parham-led Bible class sessions in Topeka, Kansas) readily preached the fullness of the Holy Spirit.

Maybe we had all hoped these racist times were in the past. They are not. Maybe we thought Nelson Mandela had ended the racism movement with his life-long anti-apartheid activism. Maybe we thought Mahatma Gandhi, or Martin Luther King, Jr., or Mother Teresa, or Desmond Tutu, or Rosa Parks, or Malala Yousafzai had brought an end to some degree to the humiliation of segments of society for who they are, what they represent, or the color of their skin. Clearly I will likely never truly understand what my minority friends experience on a daily basis, nor will I comprehend what it is like to live without white privilege. For that, I am sorry. But, more so, I want change.

I am grateful for my friends, many who are minorities and multi-cultural. Your simple willingness to be in my life, accepting and loving my family for who we are, makes me better. I have great respect for you. Thank you for standing tall while injustices abound. I vow to be a voice of healing to the cities and the nations to what extent I am offered. I promise to stand against prejudice, discrimination, and bigotry. I refuse to believe this is the new normal. Burning down city establishments, indescribable brutality to humankind, and protests that are destructive leaves us pleading for a touch of God in our land. The writer of Proverbs (31:8-9, NIV) challenges us with, "Speak up for those who cannot speak for themselves, for the rights of all who are destitute. Speak and judge fairly; defend the rights of the poor and needy."

While many do not know exactly what to say, it becomes easy to simply say nothing at all. But the silence is deafening. The topic is complex. I hurt when I think of black friends who surely must worry about their own sons and daughters every time their kids get behind the wheel of a car. I grieve with young black American mothers who have spoken with me about conversations they already have regularly with their children as young as eight years old about how to respond if they find themselves in a "situation" challenged by someone of authority. How can it be that we still have a society where precious children go to bed wondering about such conversations from moms and dads? I applaud law enforcement officers who are faithful, sincere, blameless leaders, protectors of society, and honorable in all their sacrifice. I call for justice for all who find themselves bound to horrific or murderous acts by those who are not.

> *I vow to be a voice of healing to the cities and the nations to what extent I am offered. I promise to stand against prejudice, discrimination, and bigotry. I refuse to believe this is the new normal.*

We all need someone to talk to. We need someone to educate us. We need to be saying to our minority friends,

> I see you. I see your beautiful God-given color. I see and hear your pain. I give you room to share your raw emotion. I join with you in creating a venue for cultural intervention and societal change. I don't want to assume things I know little of. I want to be vulnerable, humble, and teachable.

Race walls have divided America long enough. It is time the Church and her leaders speak out against social injustice. I want to show love, sympathy, and compassion. I want to be a voice of healing for the nations. I want to be a voice of healing for my Commonwealth and my city. Like so many we often do not know where to begin.

I encourage you to pause before you post.

I encourage you to consider your witness for Christ with your social media and with your actions and statements, as well as your silence.

I encourage you to realize that while you may be immovable about a subject, with every right to be so, to whom much is given much is required—that we might not become harmful to the body of Christ and a point of disunity, rather than focused purpose.

I encourage you to be a voice of healing.

I encourage you to stand against injustice.

I encourage you to use maturity, developed wisdom, and reliable responsibility in your leadership.

I encourage you to put actions to your words.

I encourage you to become a mentor to the fatherless.

I encourage you to visit and engage your neighbors of diversity and minorities.

I encourage you to begin conversations.

I encourage you to contact elected officials and demand justice be served.

I encourage you to vote.

I encourage you to thank faithful public servants and officers who do the right things and place their own lives on the line in harm's way for all of us daily.

I encourage you to not only *go* to church but to *be* the Church to a hurting world around us.

I encourage you to be a peacemaker.

I encourage you to make the extra-step efforts to befriend, support, and encourage Black and minority families in your communities.

I encourage you to learn from cultures different from that of your own.

I encourage you to listen to those who disagree with your position scripturally or otherwise.

I encourage you to do as Christ called the Church.

I encourage you to love.

There are so many things that can be done to make a difference. I know, for me, it begins with listening and prayer.

I cannot condone the violence, the burnings, the pointless deaths caused from such vehement riots, or the illegal looting from rage, but I can protest injustice. Leonard Ravenhill said something to the effect that most Protestant Christians are no longer Protestant, just non-Catholics; they no longer protest anything. I stand as a voice against injustice. I cannot be silent on sin. I cannot be silent on murder. I cannot be silent on senseless racism. A friend of mine said recently that violence was a face of oppression. I am praying the oppressed have a voice and the silent hear the cries. I admit I will never understand what it means to be a black man, a black husband, a black father raising children in today's America. But I will be a voice. I am going to acknowledge openly that racial discrimination is real. I am going to admit openly that there is still racism and prejudice in many pews of American Christianity. I am going to admit the Church must lead the conversation of racial reconciliation and begin with repentance.

> *I cannot condone the violence, the burnings, the pointless deaths caused from such vehement riots, or the illegal looting from rage, but I can protest injustice.*

I've visited both the location of the Azusa Street Mission and William Seymour's Los Angeles Bonnie Brae Street house-church where on April 9, 1906 seven sincere souls, worshiping with all they had within themselves, were filled with the Holy Spirit. Little did they know that this unexpected and quite unknown experience, except for what they had read in Scripture, would spark a movement around the world that was as multicultural as was ever experienced on earth.

If we ever needed a fresh Pentecost, we need it today. The promise is not for some, not for a so-called elite class, not for a people of a specific race or color, but "...for all whom our Lord our God will call" (Acts 2:39).

Chapter 10

The Prayer

> *"Yours, O Lord, is the greatness and the power and the glory and the victory and the majesty, for all that is in the heavens and in the earth is yours. Yours is the kingdom, O Lord, and you are exalted as head above all"*
> *(I Chronicles 29:11, ESV).*

I lift my voice to worship, You. You are all that I want. If it weren't for mercy and grace, oh where would I be? To be near you, Lord, I hunger. To have you near me, Lord, I wait. In You, I find my hoping, my longing, and my faith.

    Lord, I receive Your love. I receive Your light. You, O Lord, are the love of my life. I thank You, Father, that You know my name. I want to be more like You. There is no one like You, Jesus, no one like You. It is You that I take shelter. Something happens when I pause in that quiet place and just say Your name. Where You are, I am made whole. You make me whole, again. You are infinitely holy and just. You are awe-inspiringly all-powerful. You are not only great. You are noble, worthy, blameless, decent, and intrinsically good. And You, Lord, are truth. I give you my heart and I know that Your mercy is waiting. Open my eyes, O Lord, that I may see as You see, know as You know, understand as You understand, and feel as You feel. I surrender, and I surrender all.

Wrap me in Your arms, O God. Give ear to my words, O Lord. In the morning, I seek You. I commit my prayer to You. Consider my meditations. May they be a sweet, sweet sound to Your ears. I need You more day by day. I am lost without Your cause. When my strength is hard to find, You give me a sea of grace. When at times the way is lonely, the hills are steep with pain, in You I find my refuge. In You, I find my way. I want to withhold nothing from You. Holy Spirit, You are welcome in every corner of my heart. Every morning when I awaken, You deserve the glory, honor, and the praise. I cannot make it without You. I look to You, Lord Jesus, to lead my way. There are 10,000 reasons for me to sing your praise. I enter Your courts with praise. You are perfect in every way. You are righteous to me in my every misstep and heartbreak. You are loyal. You are giving. You are a friend of sinners. You are the Healer. You are my Father, God. You are my peace and my Peacemaker. You lead my steps when I am empty and unfilled. I bow before You and call You worthy. Open my eyes, Lord. Open my ears, Lord. Help me to listen.

You are so beautiful to me. I am a broken vessel. When I lose my direction, You bring me joy. When my words are scattered and my thoughts are empty, when I don't know where to start and I've never felt so down before, I come boldly to Your presence and there find Your faithfulness, Your truth, Your holy word, Your grace, still amazing. Because of who You are, I have found in You my house of prayer. When I cannot find a word to say, You have the words. I just say Your name, the name above all names. There is nothing like Your presence. You calm my fears. You dry my tears. Your lovingness changes my unworthiness. When the sun shines no more and the rain seems to never cease, You bring me new life again. When my rhythm is off, and my harmonies are refrained, You are my daily bread. You are the chord who again brings every color of the rainbow to my heart and soul. Let Your song rise in me again. In that day when forever looms before me, when my days are few, and my time has come, fill my soul with Your unending holiness. You are my hope and stay.

Your hand leads my way. I offer You my life. Set me where You will. One day without You leaves me yearning for You yet

The Prayer

again. Every worldly desire grows dim, and I wait for You. Lord, all my strength is found in standing before You. I patiently wait. I call to the deep. I search within. I seek Your face. Every step I take, I know that Your mercy awaits me. I pray, Holy Spirit, that You lead me to the love of my life. Fill me until I overflow. Breathe on me, Lord. Just breathe upon me. Your love is undeniable. Your peace calls me deeper. When my song is gone, and my step is slow, I find in You my open door. There is no name more beautiful than Jesus. You are the reason I can live. Jesus, I believe. Jesus, I trust in You. In You, I am a fruitful vine, a vine whose branches climb over a wall. You are the hope I cling to. You mean more than this world to me. You are the hand of the mighty One of Jacob. You are my Shepherd, my Rock of Israel. You are the Son of God, the Son of Man, the Bread of Life, and the Captain of the Host of the Lord. Father, You alone are Holy. You are my Deliverer. I lay my life before You. I will boast in You, alone. Your righteousness and mercy reigns.

When my dreams are on the floor, and the hopes I have believed become delusions, daydreams, and past imaginations, You are my Door. When I face crossroads of life's most important decisions, You lead me to the Rock that is higher than I. You fill my heart with songs of deliverance. You are my secret place, my hiding place, and my sanctuary. In Your presence I am made new. Nothing remains the same when it is touched by You. Touch me, Lord. You are my Advocate and the Author and the Finisher of my faith. You preserve me within Your reach. You are the Light of the world. Shine, Lord, on me. You are the Prince of Kings, the Prince of Life, and the Prince of Peace. You are the Prophet, my Redeemer, and Savior of all. You are the Guardian of my soul. Behold, what manner of love You have given to me. You are the Heir of all things. Nothing matches my time filled in You. You are the King of the ages, the King of the Jews, and the King of Kings. Take Your rightful place in my life. You are Messiah, my King, Mighty God, and Morning Star. Let the nations see grace and mercy. You give beauty for ashes, strength for fears, joy in the mourning and son-shine in the morning dew. You turn my despair to walking in victory. Only in You can I be strong. Your power within me defeats giants of today's battles. Your grace, Your amazing grace, still flows from Your throne. I give You thanks with a grateful heart. As I drink Your cup, as I eat Your bread, I honor You. I remember You and Your covenant with me. I love You, Lord. You have been so good to me.

From the shadows of my steps to Your brightness, You consume all my darkness. Fill me with Your glory, and set my heart aflame. Let Your flowing river refresh me in cleansing water. Forgive my sins, and keep them near the foot of Your Cross and at the door of Your rolled away stone. Hear my prayer, O Lord. Here I am, Lord. I will serve You. Blessed Jesus, there is no other name as Yours.

Wherever I walk, O Lord, I fear not. I carry promises of Your angels about me. I am Your steward. I place myself in Your trusted hands. Let me be Your servant. You are my Shepherd. Full or empty with all or little, I worship Your holy Name. My journey calls to You. Father, prepare me that I might be a vessel for You and Your Church. I give You all of my attention. I worship You alone. Your grace is still amazing to me. Thank You for walking with me. You comfort me. Surely goodness, love, and mercy will follow me wherever I go. How lovely is Your Name. Your gifts in Renee, Steven, Rachel, Julia, and James are the deepest earthly affections of my heart. My soul sings of Your praise. I look to You. You are worthy. You are worthy to receive my praise.

~~~~~~~~~~

In 1873, Fanny Crosby penned these words (Public Domain) of her walk of faith taken from Hebrews 10:22 and Philippians 1:21:

1. Blessed assurance, Jesus is mine!
   Oh, what a foretaste of glory divine!
   Heir of salvation, purchase of God,
   Born of His Spirit, washed in His blood.

   Refrain:
   This is my story, this is my song,

Praising my Savior all the day long;
This is my story, this is my song,
Praising my Savior all the day long.

2. Perfect submission, perfect delight,
Visions of rapture now burst on my sight;
Angels, descending, bring from above
Echoes of mercy, whispers of love.

3. Perfect submission, all is at rest,
I in my Savior am happy and blest,
Watching and waiting, looking above,
Filled with His goodness, lost in His love.

And, in the mid-1700s the commanding words of John Wesley[108] gave us his forever prayer:

> Lord Jesus, if you will receive me into your house, if you will but own me as your servant, I will not stand upon term; impose upon me what conditions you please, write down your own articles, command me what you will, put me to anything you see as good; let me come under your roof, let me be your servant ... make me what you will, Lord set me where you will. ... I put myself wholly into your hands: put me to what you will, rank me with whom you will; put me to doing, put me to suffering, let me be employed for you, or laid aside for you, exalted for you, or trodden under foot for you; let me be full, let me be empty, let me have all things, let me have nothing, I freely and heartily resign all to your pleasure and disposal.

This is my story.

Resources

Chapter 2: Cane Ridge Revival

Anderson, Gordon. *A Theology of Revival.* Minneapolis, MN: North Central Bible College, 1997.

Author Unknown. *The Cane Ridge Meeting House—James Richard Rogers and Barton Warren Stone and William Rogers.* Memphis, TN: General Books, 2012.

Campbell, Duncan. *The Lewis Awakening.* Edinburgh, Scotland: The Faith Mission, 1954.

Cane Ridge Meeting House, "The Great Revival." Accessed April 12, 2015. http://www.caneridge.org/revival.html.

Cartwright, Peter. *Autobiography of Peter Cartwright: The Backwoods Preacher.* Edited by W. P. Strickland. Cincinnati, OH: L. Swormstedt and A. Poe for the Methodist Episcopal Church, 1859.

Conkin, Paul K. *Cane Ridge: America's Pentecost.* Madison: University of Wisconsin Press, 1990.

Edwards, Brian. *Revival: A People Saturated with God.* Darlington, England: Evangelical Press, 2013.

Fish, H. C. *Handbook of Revivals.* Harrison, VA: Gano Books, 1988.

Galli, Mark. "Revival at Cane Ridge." *Christian History Magazine.* Accessed April 12, 2015. https://www.christianhistoryinstitute.org/magazine/article/revival-at-cane-ridge/.

Graves, Dan. "Strange Behavior at Cane Ridge." Christianity.com. Last modified April 2007. Accessed April 21, 2015. http://www.christianity.com/church/church-history/timeline/1801-1900/strange-behavior-at-cane-ridge-11630338.html.

McNemar, Richard. *The Kentucky Revival.* Chicago: Great Plains Press and Michael D. Fortner, 2012.

Murray, Iain. *Revival and Revivalism: The Making and Marring of American Evangelicalism 1750-1858.* Carlisle, PA: Banner of Truth Trust, 1996.

Ravenhill, Leonard. *Revival God's Way: A Message for the Church.* Bloomington, MN: Bethany House, 2006.

Shaw, S. B. *The Great Revival in Wales.* Jawbone Digital, 2012. Kindle.

Williams, D. Newell. *Barton Stone: A Spiritual Biography.* St. Louis, MO: Chalice Press, 2000.

Chapter 3: Asbury College

Apologetics Group. "The 1970 Revival at Asbury." Accessed June 17, 2015. http://theapologeticsgroup.com/product/a-revival-account-asbury-1970/.

Asbury University Archives. "The Asbury College 1970 Revival." Accessed June 17, 2015. https://www.asbury.edu/offices/library/archives/history/revivals.

"Hughes Auditorium." Accessed June 17, 2015. http://www.asbury.edu/offies/library/archives/traditions/hughes-auditorium.

Asbury University Archives, "Asbury College Revival 1970: to GOD Be the Glory."

Prather, Paul. "Asbury's Sweet, Sweet Spirit." *The Asbury Herald,* Summer 1991.

Ask.com. "Asbury College Revivals." Accessed June 17, 2015. http://search.tb.ask.com/search/GCweb.jhtml?st=bar&ptb=040D5DD2-81E2-4A69-9CE7-15F9CC748 0B7&n=781b1717&ind=2015041303&p2=^UX^xdm963^YYA ^us&si=CD15543_26-0T3SNu8M2w1D1QKQlyDQ&searchfor-=asbury+revival&pn=2&ots=1434547357171&ots=1434547359046.

Campbell, Duncan. *The Nature of a God-Sent Revival.* Vinton, VA: Christlife Publishers, 1993.

Christianity Today. "Asbury Revival Blazes Cross-Country

Trail." March 13, 1970. Accessed November 23, 2020. https:// www.christianitytoday.com/ct/1970/march-13/asbury-revival-blazes-cross-country-trail.html.

Coleman, Robert E. *One Divine Moment: The Asbury Revival.* Old Tappan, NJ: Fleming H. Revell Company, 1970.

Collier, Phillip Bruce. "The Significance of the Asbury Revival of 1970 for Some Aspects of the Spiritual Lives of the Participants." D.Min. diss., Asbury Theological Seminary, Wilmore, Kentucky, 1995.

Edwards, Brian. *Revival: A People Saturated with God.* Darlington, England: Evangelical Press, 2013.

Evans, Robert. "If My People ... A Study Guide to the Themes in Second Chronicles 7:14 for Individual or Group Use." Accessed June 17, 2015. http://revivals.arkangles.com/study-ifmypeople.php.

Fish, H. C. *Handbook of Revivals.* Harrison, VA: Gano Books, 1988.

Forerunner.com. "Asbury Revival 1970." Accessed June 17, 2015. http://forerunner.com/forerunner/X0585_Asbury_Revival_1970.html.

Gehring, Suzanne. Personal interview at Asbury University Library, June 19, 2015.

Groen, Ken. Telephone interview at Kentucky Assemblies of God offices in Crestwood, Kentucky, June 18, 2015.

Grubb, Norman. *Continuous Revival.* Fort Washington, PA: CLC Publications, 1974.

Hughes, John Wesley. *The Autobiography of John Wesley Hughes.* Louisville, KY: Pentecostal Publishing Company, 1923.

Kinlaw, Dennis. "Witness a Revival First Hand." Accessed June 17, 2015. http://archive.org/details/ RevivalFilmOfThe1970RevivalAtAsburyCollegeInKentuckyUsa.

"I am a Liar. Now What Do I Do?" Accessed June 17, 2015. https://onecanhappen.wordpress.com/2008/01/30/asbury-revival-1970-dr-kinlaw-i-am-a-liar-now-what-do-i-do/.

Kumar, Anugrah. *"Can God Bring Another Revival to America? Greg Laurie Asks."* Christian Post. Accessed June 17, 2015. http://www.christianpost.com/news/can-god-bring-another-revival-to-america-greg-laurie-asks-102061/.

MacRobert, Iain. *The Black Roots and White Racism of Early Pentecostalism in the USA.* London, England: The MacMillan Press, 1988.

McKee, Earle Stanley. *"The Early History of Asbury College, 1890-1910."* M.A. thesis, University of Kentucky, Lexington, KY, 1926.

Morrison, Henry Clay. *Some Chapters of My Life Story.* Louisville, KY: Pentecostal Publishing Company, 1941.

Murphy, Owen. *When God Stepped Down from Heaven.* Dixon. MO: Rare Christian Books, 2012.

Murray, Iain. *Revival and Revivalism: The Making and Marring of American Evangelicalism 1750-1858.* Carlisle, PA: Banner of Truth Trust, 1996.

Orr, Edwin J. *"The Welsh Revival of 1904-05."* Accessed June 17, 2015. http://onecanhappen.wordpress.com/2011/01/15/the-welsh-revival-of-1904-05-by-j-edwin-orr-a-countrywide-asbury-college-like-revival-the-4-points-1-confess-any-known-sin-and-put-any-wrong-done-to-man-right-again-2-put-away-any-doubtful-hab/.

Ravenhill, Leonard. *Revival God's Way: A Message for the Church.* Bloomington, MN: Bethany House, 2006.

Why Revival Tarries. Minneapolis: Bethany House, 1979.

Reid, Alvin. *"Revivals."* Accessed June 17, 2015. http://alvinreid.com/?p=4100.

Senapatiratne, Kevin. *Charles Finney's Lectures on Revival: Selected Messages to Ignite You, Your Church and Community.* Blaine, MN: Christ Connection Media, 2014.

Sermon Index. *"I was at the ASBURY REVIVAL."* Accessed June 17, 2015. http://www.sermonindex.net/modules/newbb/viewtopic.php?topic_id=9583&forum=40.

Thacker, Joseph A. *Asbury College: Vision and Miracle.* Napanee, IN: Evangelical Press, 1990.

Wiggs, Evan. *"1970 Tuesday 3 February – Asbury College, Wilmore, Kentucky."* Accessed June 17, 2015. http://www.evanwiggs.com/revival/history/4-1950.html.

Chapter 4: King's Way Assembly

Barton, Ruth Haley. *Invitation to Solitude and Silence: Experiencing God's Transforming Presence.* Downers Grove, IL: InterVarsity, 2010.

Edwards, Brian H. *Revival: A People Saturated with God.* Darlington, England: EP Books, 2013.

Freeman, Philip. *St. Patrick of Ireland: A Biography.* New York, NY: Simon & Schuster, 2005.

Freidzon, Claudio. *Holy Spirit, I Hunger for You.* Orlando, FL: Creation House, 1997.

Girdler, Joseph S. *Personal Hand-Written Journal.* Versailles, Kentucky, 1988-2004.

Grubb, Norman. *Rees Howells: Intercessor: The Story of a Life Lived for God.* Fort Washington, PA: CLC Publications, 2002.

Kilpatrick, John. *Pastor's Conference.* Sermon, Northwest Assembly of God, Dublin, Ohio, July 30, 1996.

Miller, R. Edward. *Secrets of the Argentine Revival.* Fairburn, GA: Peniel Outreach Ministries, 1999.

Murray, Iain H. *Revival & Revivalism: The Making and Marring of American Evangelicalism 1750-1858.* Carlisle PA: The Banner of Truth Trust, 1996.

Pratney, Winkie. *Revival: Principles to Change the World.* Springdale, PA: Whitaker House Publishing, 1984.

Ravenhill, Leonard. *Revival God's Way: A Message for the Church*. Minneapolis, MN: Bethany House Publishers, 1983.

Tennant, Carolyn. "Unit 2. Credibility-Developing Other-Leadership." Lecture, Assemblies of God Theological Seminary, Springfield, MO, October 22, 2013.

Tennant, Carolyn. *Toronto Blessing? Decide for Yourself*. Minneapolis, MN: North Central University, 1995.

General

Bandy, Thomas G. *Moving off the Map: A Field Guide to Changing the Congregation*. Nashville, TN: Abingdon Press, 1998.

Barna, George. *Evangelism That Works*, Ventura, CA: Regal Books, 1995.

Turnaround Churches: How to Overcome Barriers to Growth and Bring New Life to an Established Church. Ventura, CA: Regal Books, 1993.

Bruce, F. F. *The Book of Acts*, New International Commentary on the New Testament. Grand Rapids, MI: William. B. Eerdmans Publishing Co., 1988.

The Epistles to the Colossians, to Philemon, and to the Ephesians. New International Commentary on the New Testament, Grand Rapids, MI: William. B. Eerdmans Publishing Co., 1984.

Clowney, Edmund P. *The Church*, Leicester, England: Inter-Varsity Press, 1995.

Cole, Neil. *Organic Church: Growing Faith Where Life Happens*. San Francisco, CA: Jossey-Bass, 2005.

Conder, Tim. *The Church in Transition*. Grand Rapids, MI: Zondervan Publisher House, 2006.

Coutta, Edward Ramsey. *A Practical Guide for Successful Church Change*. Bloomington, IN: iUniverse, Inc. 2008.

Fields, Doug. *Purpose-Driven Youth Ministry: 9 Essential Foundations for Healthy Growth*. Grand Rapids, MI: Zondervan, 1998.

Ford, Kevin G. *Transforming Church: Bring Out the Good to Get to Great*. Carol Stream, IL: SaltRiver, 2007.

France, R. T. *The Gospel of Matthew*. New International Commentary on the New Testament. Grand Rapids, MI: William. B. Eerdmans Publishing Co., 2007.

Gelder, Graig Van. *The Missional Church in Context*. Grand Rapids, MI: William B. Eerdmans Publisher, 2007.

Getz, Gene A. *Sharpening the Focus of the Church*. Wheaton, IL: Victor Books, 1984.

The Measure of a Church. Glendale, CA: Regal Books, 1978.

Gibbs, Eddie. *ChurchNext: Quantum Changes in How We Do Ministry*. Downers Grove, IL: InterVarsity Press, 2000.

I Believe in Church Growth. Pasadena: CA: Fuller Seminary Press, 2000.

Girdler, Joseph S., *Setting the Atmosphere for the Day of Worship*. Crestwood, KY: Meadow Stream Publishing, 2019.

Setting the Atmosphere for the Day of Worship II. Crestwood, KY: Meadow Stream Publishing, 2020.

Jones, E. Stanley. *Reconstruction of the Church*. Nashville, TN: Abingdon Press, 1970.

Keener, Craig S. *The NIV Application Commentary: Revelation*. Grand Rapids, MI: Zondervan, 2000.

Lewis, Robert, and Wayne Cordeiro. *Culture Shift: Transforming Your Church from the Inside Out*. San Francisco, CA: Jossey-Bass, 2005.

Lincoln, Andrew T. *Ephesians*. Word Biblical Commentary 42. Nashville, TN: Thomas Nelson Publisher, 1990.

Macchia, Stephen A. *Becoming a Healthy Church: Ten Traits of a Vital Ministry*. Grand Rapids, MI: Baker Books, 1999.

Malphurs, Aubrey. *Pouring New Wine into Old Wineskins: How to Change a Church without Destroying It*. Grand Rapids, MI: Baker Books, 1993.

A New Kind of Church: Understanding Models of Ministry for the 21st Century. Grand Rapids, MI: Baker Books, 2007.

Values-Driven Leadership. Grand Rapids, MI: Baker Books, 2004.

Maxwell, John C. *Developing the Leader Within You*. Nashville, TN: Thomas Nelson, Inc., 1993.

McIntosh, Gary L. *Church That Works*. Grand Rapids, MI: Baker Pub Group, 2004.

Mounce, Robert H. *The Book of Revelation*: The New International Commentary on the New Testament. Grand Rapids, MI: William B. Eerdmans Publishing Company, 1997.

Neighbour, Ralph Webster, *Seven Last Words of the Church*. Grand Rapids, MI: Zondervan Publisher House, 1973.

Oak, John Han Hum. *Called to Awaken the Laity*. Seoul, South Korea: Duranno Press, 1984.

Rainer, Thom S. *Breakout Churches*. Grand Rapids: MI, Zondervan, 2005.

The Book of Church Growth: History, Theology, and Principles. Nashville, TN: B&H Publishing Group, 1993.

Reeder, Harry L. III. *From Embers to a Flame*. Phillipsburg, NJ: P&R Publishing, 2008.

Robinson, Anthony B. *Transforming Congregational Culture*. Grand Rapids, MI: William B. Eerdmans Publisher, 2003.

Robinson, Anthony B., and Robert W. Wall. *Called to Be Church: The Book of Acts for a New Day*. Grand Rapids, MI: William B. Eerdmans Publishing Company, 2006.

Saucy, Robert L. *The Church in God's Program*. Chicago, IL: Moody Press, 1972.

Schwarz, Christian A. *Natural Church Development: A Guide to Eight Essential Qualities of Healthy Churches*. Carol Stream: Church Smart Resources, 1996.

Southerland, Dan. *Transitioning: Leading Your Church through Change*. Grand Rapids, MI: Zondervan, 1999.

Stedman, Ray C. *Body Life: The Church Comes Alive*. Ventura, CA: Regal Books, 1972.

Stetzer, Ed, and Mike Dodson. *Comeback Churches*. Nashville, TN: B&H Publishing Group, 2007.

Planting Missional Churches. Nashville, TN: B&H Publishing Group, 2006.

Stott, John R. W. *Christian Mission in the Modern World*. Downers Grove, IL: InterVarsity, 1975.

What Christ Thinks of the Church: An Exposition of Revelation 1-3. Grand Rapids, MI: Eerdmans, 1958.

Van Gelder, Craig. *Essence of the Church: A Community Created by the Spirit*. Grand Rapids, MI Baker Books, 2000.

Wagner, C. Peter. *The Healthy Church*. Ventura, CA: Regal Books, 1996.

Wagner, Glenn E., and Steve Halliday. *The Church You've always Wanted*. Grand Rapids, MI: Zondervan, 2002.

Warren, Rick. *The Purpose Driven Church: Growth without Compromising Your Message & Mission*. Grand Rapids, MI: Zondervan Publishing House, 1995.

Willmington Harold L. *Willmington's Bible Handbook*. Wheaton, IL Tyndale House Publishers, Inc. 1997

Wood, Gene. *Leading Turnaround Churches*. St. Charles, IL: Church Smart Resources, 2001.

About the Author
Joseph S. Girdler, DMin

Superintendent, Kentucky Assemblies of God (USA)

Education

University of Kentucky, 1984

BA, Psychology

BA, Communications

Asbury Theological Seminary, 1991

MA, Missions & Evangelism

Evangel University/Assemblies of God Theological Seminary, 2018, D.Min.

Married

Pastor Joe married Renee (Dr. Renee Vannucci Girdler) on June 7, 1986. She was his birthday present, as it was also his 24th birthday. Renee is the daughter of Assemblies of God pastors from eastern Kentucky. Both parents were 100% Italian, with grandparents on both sides of her family migrating to the United States from Italy in the early 1900s.

Having served as chief resident in Family Medicine and graduating from the University of Kentucky Medical School with honors, Renee is a board-certified family medicine physician with Norton Healthcare Systems in Louisville. She is the former clinic director and vice chair of the Department of Family Medicine at the University of Louisville, as well as the former director of Clinical Affairs and vice chair of the Department of Family Medicine at the University of Kentucky. Her specialties include Women's Health Care and Diabetes, while having further interactions, as well, with International Medicine.

With an extensive background in ministry, she was previously honored by the former general superintendent of the Assemblies of God, Rev. Thomas Trask, and former AG World

Missions director, Rev. John Bueno, by her selection as the first female in Assemblies of God history appointed to the World Missions Board of the Assemblies of God. She was honored by former general superintendent, Dr. George O. Wood, in receiving the General Superintendent's Medal of Honor, the Fellowship's highest honor for lay individuals in the Assemblies of God (received at General Council 2011, Phoenix, Arizona). Renee was a longtime member of the Board of Directors for Central Bible College and Evangel University. Renee's medical and missions travels/ministries have included Ecuador, Peru, Argentina, France, Spain, Mexico, South Africa, and Belgium.

Personal

Born: Corbin, Kentucky, June 7, 1962

High School: Laurel County High School, London, Kentucky. President of Beta Club, 2-year inductee to the Kentucky All-State Concert and Symphonic Bands

College: Graduate of the University of Kentucky, 1980–1984; 4-year Music Scholarship recipient (trumpet), President UK Band, Vice-President Psi Chi, Mortar Board

Married: Dr. Renee V. Girdler, 1986

Children: Steven Joseph Girdler, MD, born 1991 (wife, Julia). Steven is a physician at Mt. Sinai Medical Center, New York, NY, Orthopedic Surgery.

Children: Rachel Renee Girdler, MSW, born 1995. Rachel is a missionary associate, Ecuador.

Grandchildren: James Hayes Girdler, born 2019, New York, NY

Presented "Mayor's Key to the City" – Versailles, Kentucky, 2004.

Approximately fifty international missions trips

Commissioned Kentucky Colonel, by Kentucky Governor Martha Layne Collins, 1986.

Commissioned Kentucky Colonel, by Kentucky Governor Matt Bevin, 2016.

About the Author

Ministry

Superintendent: Kentucky Assemblies of God, 2004–Present

General Presbyter: Assemblies of God USA, 2004–Present

General Council Assemblies of God USA, Commission on Chaplaincy, (2019-2020)

General Council Assemblies of God USA, Commission on Ethnicity, (2014-2015)

General Council Assemblies of God USA, Commission on Evangelism, (2005-2006)

District Missions Director: Kentucky Assemblies of God, (1997–2005)

Ordained: Assemblies of God, Kentucky District Council, 1994

Senior/Lead Pastor: King's Way Assembly of God, Versailles, Kentucky, (1992–2004)

Associate Pastor, Music, Youth: King's Way Assembly of God, Versailles, Kentucky, (1988–1992)

Chi-Alpha College Campus Associates: Morehead State University, Morehead, Kentucky, (1987–1988)

Publications

Girdler, Joseph S. "Royal Rangers Leaders You Are Appreciated." *High Adventure: The Official Magazine of Royal Rangers*, Summer 2006, 12-13.

Girdler, Joseph S., ed., *75th Anniversary: Kentucky District Council Assemblies of God – 2009*. Crestwood, KY: Kentucky Assemblies of God, 2009.

Girdler, Joseph S. *A Christian's Pilgrimage: Israel*. http://www.blurb.com/b/6869906-a-christian-s-pilgrimage-israel

ISBN 9781364411534, Blurb Publishing, 2016.

Girdler, Joseph S. "The Superintendent Leader-Shift from Pastoral to Apostolic Function: Awareness and Training in

Leadership Development for District Superintendents in the Assemblies of God USA." D.Min. proj., Assemblies of God Theological Seminary, Springfield, MO, 2018.

Girdler, Joseph S., and Carolyn Tennant. *Keys to the Apostolic and Prophetic: Embracing the Authentic and Avoiding the Bizarre.* Crestwood, KY: Meadow Stream Publishing, 2019.

Girdler, Joseph S. *Redemptive Missiology in Pneumatic Context.* Crestwood, KY: Meadow Stream Publishing, 2019.

Girdler, Joseph S. *Setting the Atmosphere for the Day of Worship.* Crestwood, KY: Meadow Stream Publishing, 2019.

Girdler, Joseph S. *Estableciendo La Atmósfera Para El Día De Adoración.* Crestwood, KY: Meadow Stream Publishing, 2019.

Girdler, Joseph S. *Setting the Atmosphere for the Day of Worship II.* Crestwood, KY: Meadow Stream Publishing, 2020.

Girdler, Joseph S. *Revival, Racism, & Rapture: A Fireside Reflection on Culture and Times* Crestwood, KY: Meadow Stream Publishing, 2021.

A Brief Bio

Raised Southern Baptist and Missionary Baptist, and then attending a primarily Methodist seminary, "Pastor Joe" began his ministry on a college campus serving Morehead State University in Morehead, KY, with the Assemblies of God campus ministry, Chi Alpha. Followed by four years of music ministry and youth ministry, he was propelled to a lead pastorate in 1992. His welcoming relationships with pastors of multiple fellowships and denominations have served him well in developing a broad and ecumenical approach to church networks globally. Early in ministry he was asked to serve in statewide denominational leadership. Serving initially as the Kentucky Assemblies of God World Missions director for seven years while simultaneously pastoring King's Way Assembly in the Lexington, KY, area for a total of sixteen years, Pastor Joe was then elected as the Kentucky Assemblies of God district superintendent in 2004.

About the Author

Initially a revitalization project, his pastorate with the King's Way congregation found the church overcoming paramount obstacles from the onset, but then underwent three building programs and grew to an average attendance of 400+ people. A key element was that the church grew their missional stewardship from about $15,000 to an annual missions giving of over $430,000 in only twelve years. The last year of his pastorate (2003) the church attained more than $1,000 per person, per capita missions giving, over and above the church's regular tithes and offerings. The church was honored, of well over 12,000 Assemblies of God USA congregations at that time, to achieve Top 100 status in Assemblies of God World Missions giving. Their ministry site by that time of almost forty acres and assets of approximately $4 to $5 million at the time of his transition had become one of the strongest Assemblies of God congregations in the Kentucky Assemblies of God, baptizing new converts during the morning worship service nearly every Sunday. The church's academic childcare ministry (King's Way Academy) was at the time one of the largest in the region with over 150 children five days per week and a full-time staff of over 25 leaders.

Drs. Joseph and Renee Girdler both serve (present and previous) on numerous boards and committees throughout the Assemblies of God Fellowship. Their unique journey of together integrating both ministry and medicine has offered numerous opportunities to encourage next-generational leadership in the callings of God. Of many global travels, his missions ministries have included Argentina, Peru, Ecuador (over twenty times), Mexico, El Salvador, Brazil, Italy, Germany, Austria, Spain, France, Belgium, England, Turkey, Bulgaria, Egypt, and more.

Contact Information:
Email: jgirdler@kyag.org
Website: www.joegirdler.com
Crestwood, KY 40014, USA

Also by the Author

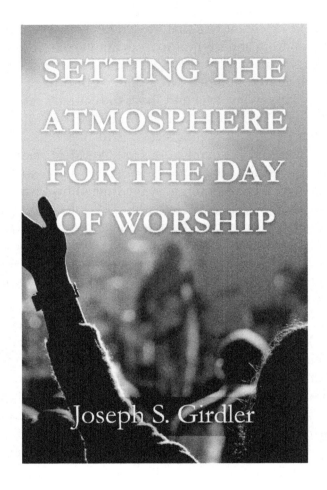

Setting the Atmosphere for the Day of Worship
ISBN: 978-1-7337952-0-3

Also by the Author

Estableciendo La Atmósfera Para El Día De Adoración
ISBN: 978-1-7337952-6-5

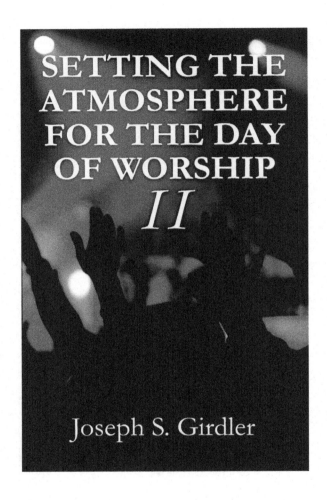

Setting the Atmosphere for the Day of Worship ll
ISBN: 978-1-7337952-8-9

Also by the Author

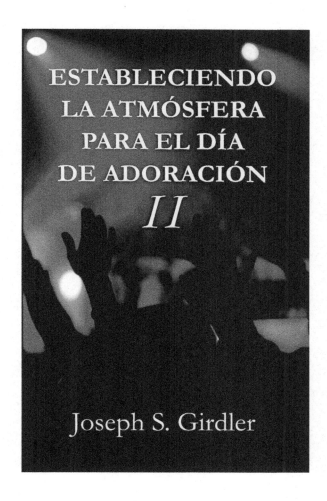

Estableciendo La Atmósfera Para El Día De Adoración ll
ISBN: 978-1-7379913-2-8

Estableciendo La Atmósfera Para El Día De Adoración l y ll
ISBN: 978-1-7379913-0-4

Also by the Author

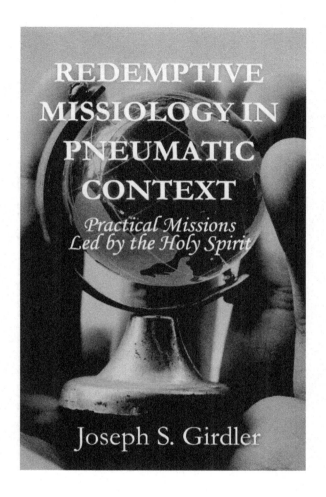

Redemptive Missiology in Pneumatic Context

ISBN: 978-1-7337952-2-7

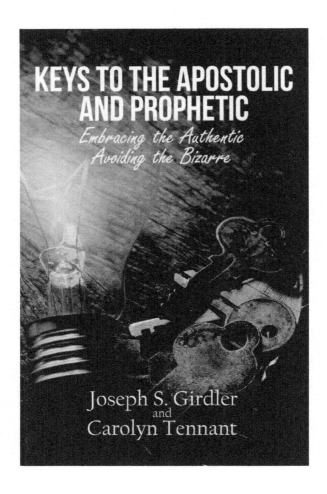

Keys to the Apostolic and Prophetic:
Embracing the Authentic - Avoiding the Bizarre
ISBN: 978-1-7337952-4-1

Endnotes

Chapter 2
1 Gordon Anderson, *A Theology of Revival* (Minneapolis, MN: North Central Bible College, 1997), 63.
2 Cane Ridge Meeting House, accessed April 12, 2015, http://www.caneridge.org.
3 Iain Murray, *Revival and Revivalism: The Making and Marring of American Evangelicalism 1750-1858* (Carlisle, PA: Banner of Truth Trust, 1996), 145.
4 Cane Ridge Meeting House, accessed April 12, 2015, www.caneridge.org.
5 D. Newell Williams, *Barton Stone: A Spiritual Biography* (St. Louis, MO: Chalice Press, 2000), 59.
6 Ibid., 60.
7 Ibid., 59.
8 Ibid., 60.
9 Cane Ridge Meeting House, accessed April 12, 2015, www.caneridge.org.
10 S. B. Shaw, *The Great Revival in Wales* (Jawbone Digital, 2012), loc. 87, 92, Kindle.
11 Dan Graves, "Strange Behavior at Cane Ridge," Christianity.com, last modified April 2007, accessed April 21, 2015, http://www.christianity.com/church-history/timeline/1801-1900/strange-behavior-at-cane-ridge-11630338.html.
12 Richard McNemar, *The Kentucky Revival* (Chicago: Great Plains Press and Michael D. Fortner, 2012), 23.
13 Leonard Ravenhill, *Revival God's Way: A Message for the Church* (Bloomington, MN: Bethany House, 2006), 35.
14 Peter Cartwright, *Autobiography of Peter Cartwright: The Backwoods Preacher*, ed. W. P. Strickland (Cincinnati, OH: L. Swormstedt and A. Poe for the Methodist Episcopal Church, 1859), 30.
15 Murray, *Revival and Revivalism*, 158.
16 McNemar, *The Kentucky Revival*, 26.
17 Ibid., *The Kentucky Revival*, 125.

18 Ibid., *The Kentucky Revival*, 132.
19 McNemar, *The Kentucky Revival*, 12.
20 Brian Edwards, *Revival: A People Saturated with God* (Darlington, England: Evangelical Press, 2013), 265.
21 Williams, *Barton Stone: A Spiritual Biography*, 63.
22 Ibid., 62.
23 Edwards, *Revival*, 246-247.
24 Williams, *Barton Stone: A Spiritual Biography*, 150.
25 Ibid., 139.
26 Ibid., 160.
27 Williams, *Barton Stone: A Spiritual Biography*, 57.
28 Graves, "Strange Behavior."
29 Williams *Barton Stone: A Spiritual Biography*, 26.
30 Ibid.
31 Ibid., 49.
32 Ibid., 34.
33 Ibid.
34 "Kentucky Revival," February 10, 2004, Send Revival, accessed April 12, 2015, http://www.sendrevival.com/Kentucky Revival.
35 Ibid.
36 Williams, *Barton Stone: A Spiritual Biography*, 51.
37 Paul K. Conkin, *Cane Ridge: America's Pentecost* (Madison: University of Wisconsin Press, 1990), 59.
38 Ibid., 60.
39 Graves, "Strange Behavior."
40 Williams, *Barton Stone: A Spiritual Biography*, 19.
41 Conkin, *Cane Ridge: America's Pentecost*, 53.
42 Williams, *Barton Stone: A Spiritual Biography*, 21.
43 Williams, *Barton Stone: A Spiritual Biography*, 21.
44 Ibid.
45 Duncan Campbell, *The Lewis Awakening* (Edinburgh, Scotland: The Faith Mission, 1954), 30.
46 Cartwright, *Autobiography of Peter Cartwright*, 48.
47 McNemar, *The Kentucky Revival*, 68.
48 H. C. Fish, *Handbook of Revivals* (Harrisonburg, VA: Gano

Books, 1988), 17.
49 Ibid., 18.
50 Cartwright, *Autobiography of Peter Cartwright*, 51.
51 Fish, *Handbook of Revivals*, 19.
52 Ibid., 245.
53 Murray, *Revival and Revivalism*, 170.
54 Ibid.
55 J. D. Douglas, Walter A. Elwell, and Peter Toon, eds., *The Concise Dictionary of the Christian Tradition* (Grand Rapids, MI: Zondervan, 1989), 326.

Chapter 3
56 Taken from Commonwealth of Kentucky, Historical Society, Department of Highways road sign in front of Asbury University. Viewed June 19, 2015.
57 Ibid.
58 Asbury University Archives, "Asbury College Revival 1970: To GOD Be the Glory."
59 Ask.com, "Asbury College Revivals," accessed June 17, 2015.
60 Ibid. "Asbury's Sweet, Sweet Spirit" by Paul Prather. The Asbury Herald, Summer 1991.
61 Ibid.
62 "Asbury Revival Blazes Cross-Country Trail," *Christianity Today*, March 13, 1970.
63 Asbury University Archives, "Asbury College Revival 1970: To GOD Be the Glory."
64 Ibid.
65 Suzanne Gehring, (personal interview, Asbury University Library, Wilmore, Kentucky, June 19, 2015).
66 Leonard Ravenhill, *Revival God's Way: A Message for the Church* (Minneapolis: Bethany House Publishers, 2006), 135.
67 "Asbury College Revival 1970: To GOD Be the Glory."
68 Ibid.
69 Ibid.
70 Ibid.
71 Ibid.

72 Ibid.
73 Ken Groen, personal telephone interview, Offices of Kentucky Ministry Network of the Assemblies of God, Crestwood, Kentucky, June 18, 2015.
74 Ibid.
75 Norman Grubb, *Continuous Revival* (Fort Washington, PA: Christian Literature Crusade, 1974), 26.
76 Ibid., 28-29.
77 Carolyn Tenant, "Nine Characteristics of Revival" (lecture, Assemblies of God Theological Seminary, Springfield, MO, June 9, 2015).
78 Phillip Bruce Collier, "The Significance of the Asbury Revival of 1970 for Some Aspects of the Spiritual Lives of the Participants" (D.Min. diss., Asbury Theological Seminary, Wilmore, Kentucky, 1995), 27-28.
79 Perhaps add a footnote here to refer to the reference and perhaps any other book (Tennant?) that would add more info to that phrase.
80 Groen, *Interview*.
81 Collier, "The Significance of the Asbury Revival of 1970 for Some Aspects of the Spiritual Lives of the Participants", 40.
82 Robert E. Coleman, *One Divine Moment: The Asbury Revival* (Old Tappan, NJ: Fleming H. Revell Company, 1970), 13.
83 Ibid. 32.
84 Ibid. 56.
85 Ibid.
86 Ibid., 108.

Chapter 4
87 Joseph S. Girdler, "Personal Journal," December 19, 1988.
88 Ibid., September 27, 1993.
89 Ibid., June 1, 1997.
90 John Kilpatrick, "Pastor's Conference" (sermon, Northwest Assembly of God, Dublin, Ohio, July 30, 1996).
91 Philip Freeman, *St. Patrick of Ireland: A Biography* (New York, NY: Simon & Schuster, 2005), 105.
92 Brian H. Edwards, *Revival: A People Saturated with God*

(Darlington, England: EP Books, 2013), 69.
93   Iain H. Murray, *Revival & Revivalism: The Making and Marring of American Evangelicalism 1750-1858* (Carlisle PA: The Banner of Truth Trust, 1996), 251.
94   Edwards, *Revival: A People Saturated...*, 132.
95   Girdler, "Personal Journal," June 1, 1997.
96   Leonard Ravenhill, *Revival God's Way: A Message for the Church* (Minneapolis, MN: Bethany House Publishers, 1983), 133.
97   Norman Grubb, *Rees Howells: Intercessor: The Story of a Life Lived for God* (Fort Washington, PA: CLC Publications, 2002), 132.
98   R. Edward Miller, *Secrets of the Argentine Revival* (Fairburn, GA: Peniel Outreach Ministries, 1999), 54.
99   Girdler, "Personal Journal," July 30, 1996.
100 Murray, *Revival & Revivalism*, 149-150.
101 Winkie Pratney, *Revival: Principles to Change The World* (Springdale, PA: Whitaker House Publishing, 1984), 296.
102 Claudio Freidzon, *Holy Spirit, I Hunger for You* (Orlando, FL: Creation House, 1997), 69.
103 Ibid., 69-71.
104 Carolyn Tennant, *Toronto Blessing? Decide for Yourself* (Minneapolis, MN: North Central University, 1995), 10.
105 Carolyn Tennant, "Unit 2. Credibility—Developing Other-Leadership," (lecture, Assemblies of God Theological Seminary, Springfield, MO, October 22, 2013), PowerPoint Slide 17/59.
106 Ruth Haley Barton, *Invitation to Solitude and Silence: Experiencing God's Transforming Presence* (Downers Grove, IL: InterVarsity, 2010), 128.

Chapter 7
107 Often people are confused as to the names Calvary and Golgotha. The Bible says Jesus was crucified at a spot outside Jerusalem called Golgotha, which in Aramaic means "place of the skull." The Latin word for skull is "calvaria." In English, Christians call the site of the crucifixion, Calvary.

Chapter 10
108 John Wesley, "Renewing the Covenant," in *Discipline of the*

Methodist Church of Canada (Toronto: Samuel Rose, 1874), 171-172.
https://archive.org/details/cihm_26575/page/n185/mode/2up.

Made in the USA
Monee, IL
28 February 2022

91844533R00108